RELIGION
AND THE
COMMON MAN

E. C. URWIN

RELIGION
AND THE
COMMON
MAN

SCM PRESS LTD
56 BLOOMSBURY STREET, LONDON WCI

First published January 1951

Printed in Great Britain by
Northumberland Press Limited
Gateshead on Tyne

PREFACE

AS THE PROLOGUE sets out, this book has a very personal
origin. Now that I have come to its completion, I recognize
that what I have written is simply a sketch of my working
philosophy as a Christian minister for forty years, seeking to
establish with deepening conviction the relevance of religion
midst the whirl of events in the modern world. Religion
early cast its spell upon me, and I have never been able to
shake off the assurance of its ultimate truth as the explanation of our existence, despite the rude challenges that have
sought to dislodge it. I have tested the alternatives as
thoroughly as I know how, but neither the grim, relentless
and illusory creed of atheistic Marxianism, nor the aridity of
secularism, nor the presumptions of scientific humanism
suffice me, and I turn from them to religious faith.

If I am asked for whom I have written, the answer
primarily is: for myself, to satisfy the quest that has never
let me rest, namely: what is the ultimate truth and authority
of religion? I would like to believe, however, that the result
may be of some interest to fellow-travellers in the Christian
ministry, who have pursued the quest with me; of some help
to laymen in the hurly-burly of working days, who desire
to know how relevant religion is to their wrestle with life
to-day; and, above all, to some of those of whose need of
religion, if the hopes they cherish are not to prove utterly
vain, I have especially written. Some of the things said in
this book have been tried out on many of them already.

My indebtedness to others is far beyond my power to
recount. I can only mention two or three. First, my friend
of many years, Dr. Hugh Martin, for his unfailing en-
couragement, candid criticism and acceptance of the idea of

the book before ever the book itself saw the light. Second, to two constant helpers: Miss Dorothy Bolton, my diligent and faithful secretary, who has typed the manuscript, some parts of it twice or three times over, not withholding on occasion her own frank comment; and Miss E. G. Page, who has not only read the MS., but corrected the proofs and patiently checked the number of words. Finally, my comrade of the years, who has read the MS. chapter by chapter as it took shape. She is the guardian at the gate. Had she not passed the labour of my hands, it would never have seen the light.

E. C. URWIN.

CONTENTS

PROLOGUE

I

WHY THIS BOOK, and why this title? I am myself of the stock of the common people, and rejoice in it. My father left school in a Cornish village at ten, and what learning he acquired after that was for the most part self gained. Some of his youth was spent in granite quarry and tin mine, and in the remaining years before he became a minister of the Gospel he helped to sustain a widowed mother and a family of younger sisters by delivering coal and carrying fourteen and twenty-stone bags of flour to the scattered dwellings of a hamlet on the Cornish uplands.

I can trace my ancestral roots back for two hundred years, well into the eighteenth century, and therefore know the soil from which I come: peasant farmers, quarrymen and tin miners, generation after generation, both on my father's and my mother's side. There are picturesque Celtic names along the track to prove it, like Tregonning and Trewen and farmsteads with such entrancing designations as Carvednack and Trelusback.

What is more, I have moved in and out of the homes of the common people all my life. My father's calling as a Methodist minister provided me with unique opportunities of doing so. When "travelling" in East Anglia, he often took me with him on his journeys in the Circuit trap, and that meant tea in farm-house kitchens and partaking the plain and simple fare of farm labourers' tables in Norfolk and Lincolnshire. My schooldays were spent in the schools of the people, a village school among the Cheviots, another in a West Cumberland seaport town where my school-fellows were the sons of small tradesmen, miners, iron-workers and dockers. My first occupation was as a pupil teacher in a Board School in a Lancashire industrial town, where one of my memories is the weekly duty of signing half-time books for the lads and lasses just beginning work in the mills. There followed two memorable years in another school in one of the grittiest parts of grimy Sheffield.

My own calling as a Methodist minister for over a quarter of a century was mainly fulfilled amongst working-class people. I began my ministry in the Lancashire town of Preston, where most of my people were " gradely mill-folks ". There followed twelve years in London. Six were spent in West Islington in an area of one square mile where a hundred thousand people dwelt and I hadn't a single family that lived in a whole house. The other six were lived out in a fading surburban area on the edge of theatrical Brixton, and again most of my people were working folk with a sprinkling of lower middle-class folk. Only once in my ministry have I had much to do with the big-merchant manufacturing class, and one of my reasons for accepting that call was that I might see for myself what life was like on that level. That was in Bristol. Even there I had a considerable sprinkling of working-class folk amongst my people, and I remember hearing of a remark made by one of them: "He's a working man's man!" I didn't as a matter of fact try to be anybody's man, but everybody's so far as they had need of me. The remark, however, has some significance as showing the measure of sympathy I have for those of the same stock as that from which I myself come.

My last personal charge was in a small West Riding town between Leeds and Bradford, mainly amongst wool merchants, woollen manufacturers and textile workers. I had intimate friends in every class. I learned something of the trials of men engaged in the buying and selling of wool and its preparation for manufacture. I caught glimpses of the manufacturer's struggles to get business when trade is bad,

and felt the stark nakedness of the worker's plight when
he has no work by which to earn his daily bread.

II

Twenty-five years of such experience of life amongst working folk taught me much. I learned how soul-depressing
economic poverty can be, and the furtive temper that may
be developed in the casual worker chivvied from job to job.
I fought that kind of poverty in the slums of West Islington.
I have peeped behind the scenes in fashionable West End
dress-making rooms, and caught echoes of a seamstress's life
in a Hoxton blouse factory. I have struggled with others
for a fair deal for the unemployed of a great city, and
agitated till some provision was made for their enforced
leisure in that West Riding community where I spent three
all too short years of consuming interest. With others like-
minded in the City of Bristol, I engaged in an adventure to
contribute something to the better housing of the people.

If my experience is limited at any point, it is chiefly that
I have only little first-hand knowledge of " political labour ".
I inherited from my father a political radicalism that had its
roots in the nineteenth century. Many of my working-class
friends were ardent trade unionists, and the more I learned
of the conditions of life and labour in mine, factory and
workshop, the more I understood and sympathized with
them in their struggles. The one thing in the political conflicts of Britain from 1910 on that has stirred me has been the
effort to create and develop the social services.

III

The point of all this is that this experience came to me as
a working minister of religion. Just because these were the
conditions of life of the people whom I served I had to be
interested in them, sharing their struggles, striving with
them for a larger measure of social justice, entering into

their hopes and warring with them against the frustrations which barred them from their rightful heritage in the true wealth of life. I have caught repeated glimpses of the inferiority complex in them which often reveals itself by reason of their lack of educational opportunity. Some of their awkwardness is due to that one thing. I have also seen to what heights of culture, understanding and capacity to serve the public good they can attain when given opportunity.

But my supreme interest was in finding out what religion could do for them. I was there among them as a minister of religion, to ground their life as far as I could on faith in God and to win them to the Christian way of life. I had unique opportunities of testing whether it was of any avail. Religion was the dominant interest in which I was cradled. It gave colour and intensity to life in that Cornish village from which my father and mother came, and still does, and my own life was deeply dyed with it. When the age of reflection came, my prevailing interest was to establish, at least for myself, the truth on which religion rests.

One way of doing that was to test its efficacy in the lives of those who were influenced by it. Not that they were necessarily better than other folks. They had their faults and failings, and the sins of religious people can be very unlovely. Nevertheless, the evidences of the power of religion when it was really alive were unmistakable. It could transform profligate life: I saw it do so in the lives of Cumberland miners. It could evoke devotion and purposeful character, inspire patient heroism and endurance in suffering, and develop lovely tempers and graces of the spirit, and bring forth saints in the most unlikely quarters. Of all these things, illustrative of the transforming power of religion, I could give innumerable examples.

One must suffice. In my Preston days, one of my people —a man who opened heart and home to me—followed the unsavoury occupation of skin dresser in a skin-yard, dressing the hides and skins of cattle and sheep from butchers' slaughter-houses. But William Kirton was a philosopher in embryo, and the why and wherefore of life was his perpetual quest. Many a " crack " about the ultimate questions have I had by his fireside. One such conversation led on to the subject of our discernment of spiritual reality behind the outward show of things. He went to his work in the skin-yard fired by his new discovery that " heaven was all about us ". He reported to me afterwards what had happened, how quite spontaneously conversation had sprung up be-tween the men at work at their benches, and turned on the very subject we had thrashed out at his own fireside, how work had stopped and " economics " went to the four winds, and at last silence had fallen while the wonder sank in. " Man," he said to me, " that silence was deathly. Then . . . broke in: ' Why, Bill, there must be heaven here in the skin-yard!' "

Such language will be rudely dismissed by some as mystic-ism and superstition. It was real enough to the man in question. And here is the point. " Bill ", my friend, William Kirton, had a life-long struggle with economic vicissitude and physical suffering, in facing which his faith in religion was the one abiding resource that upheld him. Nor did it fail him.

IV

I come to the issue to be faced in this book. As a later chapter will seek to demonstrate, a new era, unlike to any other in the world's history, has dawned for the common man. He has entered into political power with the right to determine his economic destiny and achieve his cultural heritage. But in the doing of it, it is claimed that he has less and less need of religion; nay more, that religion is a hind-rance to him in his struggle for liberty and justice, and is indeed one of the forces which prey upon him from which he needs to be emancipated.

Certainly the divorce of working-class Europe from the

Christian faith, so far as it is true, is a fact to be reflected upon. If there has been failure on the part of the Christian Church, failure either in loyalty to the Gospel or in sensitiveness to social justice, it must be acknowledged and the cause brought to light. This book will at least seek to be frank on that score.

But the crucial problem will remain: can the common man be emancipated, or as I prefer to say, old-fashioned though the word be, " redeemed " and attain betterment of his life and lot, without religion and the grace of God which it is the business of the Christian faith to mediate to him? If he can be so " redeemed " without religion, then the critics of religion are right: the sooner the delusion that he needs religion is dispelled and consigned to the limbo of forgotten things the better. But if the truth be that he needs religion, and cannot be " redeemed " without it—and I have the deep conviction that he cannot—then the critics must be controverted, and the truth be demonstrated that whatever else be done for the emancipation of the common man must fail and suffer frustration unless this inner need of religion is met and satisfied. To establish the truth in this matter, this book is written.

I

RELIGION AND
THE COMMON MAN

I

WHO IS THE COMMON MAN? For the moment we
define him as just one of the great mass of ordinary people
the world over; generally working with his hands for daily
bread, of undistinguished and even nameless ancestry, with
little or no property, passing through this life mid toiling
days, tasting his meed of sorrow, joy, misery, wretchedness,
folly, and because no other word fits the fact, sin. In character he is capable of great heights and squalid depths: now
succumbing to debauchery, profligacy, vice and brutishness:
now touched to finer things, fellow feeling, good companionship, loyalty, domestic felicity, or stirred to great issues, and
discerning the signs of the times with a shrewd insight.
Often class conscious, he moves most easily in the mass; but
every now and again he will be stirred by some deep resent-
ment and dumb sense of injustice to a rebellious individualism, when he can be as stubborn as a mule. Like the
rest of mankind, he is often motivated by greed and self-
interest.

The real question is how he, and the great mass of his
fellows with him, can be wooed and won out of the welter
of his instinctive passions and impulses, out of the frustration of injustice and wrong which he has suffered, out of
his own folly and wrongdoing, to a purposeful existence.
Ultimately this is what the purpose of religion will be taken

to mean in this book. Briefly it is what the New Testament means by being " reconciled to God ". Religion, so conceived as a right relation with God, is the spring of man's redemption, and it is with the common man's " redemption " that we are concerned.

We must, however, notice other lesser meanings and shades of meaning which the word " redemption " is made to bear. The word derives its original force from deliverance from slavery, serfdom and other iniquitous oppressions which have been visited upon the common man. Thus the idea of redemption bears upon his economic liberation—how can he achieve a fruitful and satisfying way of labour for the satisfaction of his economic necessities and the building up of an adequate standard of material life? But this leads into the question of political liberty; for if economics originally means the management of the household, so politics is the government of the city by which man's freedom and security are assured and justice is guaranteed. To achieve a purposeful existence on this planet man must overcome economic necessity and political disorder. This, however, involves self-conquest—victory over sloth, conquest over anarchic instinctive impulses and tumultuous passions: therefore culture of the mind, the emotions and the will. According to the ancient view, self-mastery is a mark of the good life, and no man is truly redeemed who has not achieved victory over passion and desire. So redemption gains a new shade of meaning, and stands for the achieving of spiritual culture and self-mastery.

We must also take note of the social setting in which any man will realize a purposeful existence. For it is part of the complexity of human life that man is a social being, not meant to live alone. His redemption, therefore, must include the achievement of enduring and meaningful social relationships—in family life, in neighbourhood, in industry, with people of his own race and other races, in a word, the growth of a worthy community of mankind. Individual man comes to birth in a society, the family, and the achievement of personality is through personal relations with others in a community, ever enlarging and expanding, till life becomes a network of personal relationships. He may on occasion shrink into himself, cultivate an inner circle of intimate relationships: but one mark of growth is the number of persons who mean something to him. So there can be no redemption apart from a redeemed society.

II

What are the resources of the common man for achieving such a purposeful existence, and what are the horizons of that life? Here come in some of the acutest divergences of our time as to the dimensions and worth of the common man's life, concerning which the debate waxes fast and furious. To some the human species is a creature of time and sense, a species of higher ape, with no destiny beyond the bounds of his mortality. True, he possesses some distinguishing marks, bigger brain, capacity to reason, and over-weening self-consciousness that sometimes becomes towering pride. Yet he is a creature of instinct and passion likewise, and so prone to folly, self-destruction and the doing of injury to his fellows. Both individually and corporately, he can be diabolically cruel and more savage than the great carnivora or the killer whale: yet he is capable of ranges of feeling and understanding, joy and exultation, or shame and remorse, such as, so far as we can discern, other animal species never know. But, on the view that he is but a creature of time and sense, with this world only for his domain for his short spell of life, the most that he can do is to make life as tolerable as possible while he remains here, and then pass out as though he never had been. But such a view raises the remorseless question: Why, being what he is, was he ever born? To which neither reason nor sense can make reply. On that view there is no reason for human existence: and human life is what some people say it is: illusion!

B

The opposite view widens the horizons of human destiny to eternity. This creature of time also is heir of another world. He is born for another life as well as this one. He is not only child of man; his ultimate destiny, for which life is given him, is to become a child of God. Sometimes the contrast between the two aspects of this double existence is pressed so as to make them exclusive of each other: a man, it is said, is either this-worldly or other-worldly. The antithesis, so pressed, may work either way. The this-worldly man will deny the legitimacy of the other-worldly view; the other-worldly view repudiate the obligations and validity of this one. But truth here may be paradoxical as always: and life be both this-worldly and other-worldly at the same time.

In any case, our problem becomes clear. On which view is the common man most likely to find his redemption and win his way into purposeful existence? That is the issue which we have to weigh. Each view has its advocates in the modern world. On the one hand, " the eighteenth and nine-teenth centuries assumed that if only these other-worldly hopes, which seemed to beguile man from his mundane tasks, could be disavowed, it would be possible to centre human attention so completely upon the achievement of the ' land of promise ' in this world that all of man's frustrations could be overcome ".[1] In other words, on this view our redemption belongs to time and time alone. But on the other hand, it is just as resolutely affirmed that that is a fore-shortening of man's true destiny, that if in this life only we have hope, we are doomed to frustration, with the deepest hungers of our hearts unsatisfied, and that " the life beyond this world is, in very deed, the inspiration of the life that now is ".[2]

---

[1] Reinhold Niebuhr: *Discerning the Signs of the Times*, p. 168.
[2] Ernst Troeltsch: *The Social Teaching of the Christian Churches*, Vol. II, p. 1006.

III

Nor does that exhaust the issue. It must also be faced in terms of belief or disbelief in God. Few things are clearer in the modern world than that great numbers of those who pin their faith to this world only have surrendered all belief in God or the supernatural. The very conception of God, it has been said, has dropped out of the mind of the modern man. The great historic religions are counted as disproven superstitions, which may be allowed to survive as private delusions in the minds of their adherents, but ought to be permitted no influence on public affairs. The religion of the modern man, on this view, is atheism, a bleak affair, tinged often enough with rebel bitterness, although also on occasion lit up by noble but desperate resolve to make the best of the situation. On this view, man must be his own redeemer. He is deprived, by hypothesis, of anything that can be called "the grace of God". Let it be granted that some who take this view look on the prospect undismayed. Since God is non-existent, they say, and religion irrelevant, man must look to himself alone, and, whether as collective man or super-man, they affirm, he is quite capable of achieving his own redemption without any divine resource. It may be over-towering pride, and may end in disaster, but they are prepared to try. Man, they declare, is master of his own destiny and captain of his own soul.

On the other view which has eternity for its horizons and God for its focus, this is but a braggart creed. Man's true life, the upholders of religion affirm, is in God and apart from God he is helpless. His very strength to live is God-given. He needs divine grace continually, for deeper reasons than we have yet sighted, and can be assured of it if he but trust in God. On this view, his redemption is of God and cannot be achieved apart from Him. Still more, to find his true life in God is the real goal of his existence, the purpose for which he was born. This, at any rate, is the faith of the great religions of revelation, supremely of the Christian revelation, of which the others seem but broken lights or imperfect foreshadowings, and is confirmed by the testimony of saints and prophets in all ages, to whom communion with God is the very acme of human experience, through which alone man is fitted for community with his fellows. This view finds the only sufficient ground for the love of man in the love of God, and declares therefore in resonant language that the chief end of man is to glorify God and enjoy Him for ever.

II

THE MODERN CONCERN FOR
THE COMMON MAN

THE REDEMPTION of the common man, in one or other or all of the meanings and shades of meaning indicated, has become one of the deepest ferments of the modern world. His plight has profoundly stirred the conscience of mankind, and evoked passionate protest, fiery indignation, feverish effort and revolutionary struggle again and again. Who, however, once more we ask, is the common man? The answer, sufficient for our present purpose, is: the unprivileged mass of the people everywhere and anywhere.

I

Nineteenth-century political and social debate accustomed us to the ugly word "proletariat", meaning the vast multitude of landless and propertyless men and women, heavily breeding and quickly dying, whose condition was the outcome of the Industrial Revolution, and whose only wealth was the labour of hand and brain. As the machine age came upon the world, more and more the working population was divorced from the land in which they had been rooted for centuries, herded into the towns, their labour exploited for others' gain, over-driven, under-paid, badly housed and with few of the necessary conditions for health and well-being, let alone decent amenities of life. The bitter story is well known and need not here be recapitulated. We only remind ourselves that as industrialism spread, the position of the common man became a problem and a challenge in every land. The problem arose in Great Britain where industrialism first struck its roots, and set tasks for successive generations of statesmen and reformers which even now are not fully accomplished. The surging tide of unrest spread through France and Germany and reached Russia. It swept to America, as successive waves of emigrants were caught up in the toils of American industry. It passed to the East as industrialism reached China, India and Japan, and penetrated up the Congo Valley and made its consequences felt on the Copper Belt of the Rhodesias and the Witwatersrand at Johannesburg. Amongst its reverberations are those of the oil wells of Rumania, the Caucasus and Persia.

Nor, to make our picture complete, should we forget the workers who remain upon the land. Agriculture is still the world's major industry, and one of the worst paid. Of the total population of the world to-day, it is estimated that over 1,000,000,000, or almost half, are rooted in the soil. They are, after all, our chief primary producers. A picturesque and varied host they make, ranging from rice farmers, workers on tea plantations, stock rearers, sheep farmers and wheat farmers, peasant farmers of Europe, depressed peon farmers of South America, cotton and tobacco growers of the U.S.A., cocoa growers in West Africa, and banana growers in Jamaica, together with lumber men in the great forest lands. In all these varied types we come face to face again with the common man.

The backward races, as they are called, must also be considered in the total picture. Negro slavery was a wrong perpetrated against African peoples for three centuries, creating economic and political problems for Europe and America. The opening up of Africa by the white races in the nineteenth century brought the evils of exploitation to many a primitive tribe of South Africa, the Belgian Congo and the Cameroons. Few activities scar and disfigure the record of the white races like their treatment of the black peoples of the earth.

II

As we have said, however, awakening to the plight of the common man and the grim wrongs done to him has been an outstanding characteristic of modern history. We need go no further back than those political seers who drafted the American Constitution or the man whose pregnant words helped to set in train the fierce flames of the French Revolution, Rousseau. "We hold these truths to be self-evident," declared the first, "that all men are created equal, that they are endowed by their Creator with certain unalienable Rights, that among these are Life, Liberty and the pursuit of Happiness." "Man is born free," asserted the second, "but everywhere he is in chains."

To affirm those rights and to break those chains were to be the incentives of revolutionary effort both in the political and economic fields for many a long day. The American War of Independence and the French Revolution set the pace in the one field. Of this the restless dynamic figure of "Citizen Tom Paine", as he has recently been styled, is sufficient evidence. With his *Common Sense*, he stirred the American colonists to the meaning of independence, popular government free from the caprices of monarchy, republican in form and representative in character; and with his successive *Crisis* papers, often written on drum-heads by candle-light, he kindled anew into flame the flagging spirits of Washington's army. If Burke's *Reflections on the French Revolution* served to excite a prejudice against both France and the Revolution which lasted for a generation and introduced an era of political repression, Paine's *Rights of Man*, written in reply to Burke, excited a ferment of ideas whose explosive force at last produced popular support for the Reform Bill of 1832 and the larger franchise demanded by the Chartist Movement. Somewhere in the hearts of

British working men lurked the memory of those first two
of the declarations of the National Assembly:

(i) Men are born and always continue, free and equal in
respect of their rights. . . .

(ii) The end of all political associations is the preservation
of the natural and imprescribable rights of man, and these
rights are Liberty, Property, Security, and Resistance of
Oppression.

Amid such resounding declarations of principle was
political democracy launched upon its conquest of the
modern world. We can trace its ferment all through nineteenth-century Europe, its century-long struggle for realization in Britain, its transfer to the Dominions of the British
Commonwealth, its impact on the new South American
nations, and finally in the twentieth century to Asia. Part
of the common man's redemption was his political emancipation, and the achievement, as Abraham Lincoln put it, of
government of the people, by the people and for the people.

Mingled in inextricable confusion with the political
struggle was the impulsive force of the struggle for mastery
of the economic conditions under which the common man
lived. This phase of the struggle was especially evoked by
the Industrial Revolution. In Britain there was the winning of the workers' rights of combination in demanding
just conditions in regard to wages and hours, the rise of
the trade unions, the passing of the Factory Acts and the
development of machinery for negotiation between masters
and men. As the Industrial Revolution spread to country
after country, similar developments of governmental regu-
lation of conditions of labour took place, to culminate
eventually in the patient toil of the International Labour
Office to equalize conditions in industry the world over.
Gradually also there evolved a sense of the responsibility of
government for ordering social well-being: sanitation,
water supply, street lighting and housing; and eventually
the expanding range of social services which characterize the

welfare state. Wealth gained by the labour of all must be equitably shared by all.

Alongside these prosaic though hard-won gains in organization, legislation and social services came the alluring, challenging and variegated body of ideas known as Socialism, recently reviewed so discerningly and patiently and withal with a touch of ironic humour by Alexander Gray in *The Socialist Tradition from Moses to Lenin*. There is a long history to such ideas, as the full title of Gray's book suggests, and an almost bewildering diversity in the conceptions of a reborn or remade social order to which they lead. So much we are forced to say if we compare notions associated with the names of Robert Owen, St. Simon, Fourier, Proudhon, the "utopian" socialists as they have been called, with those of professed anarchists like Bakunin and Kropotkin, and "scientific" socialism like that of the Marxists, to say nothing of French Syndicalism and the English Guild Socialists. If, following Gray, we try to find the common impulses underlying this bewildering diversity, we detect a deep discontent with economic frustration and wrong, a protest against private property in the means of production as being an instrument of oppression and exploitation, a conviction that industry should be an ordered social enterprise and, finally, a profound hunger for a more satisfying form of community life. Throughout runs passionate concern for the well-being of the common man.

III

Preoccupation with political liberty or economic emancipation, however, was not the only impulse which brought about awakening of concern for the redemption of the common man in the modern world. There was an awakening of quite remarkable force from the side of the Christian religion, finding its origin most clearly in the Evangelical Revival in eighteenth-century England. The consequences of this have recently been described afresh by the American historian Latourette in his *History of the Expansion of Christianity*, and his smaller book *The Unquenchable Light*.

The essential characteristics of the Evangelical Revival need only briefly be recalled. Rising in eighteenth-century England in an age when Deism had made God remote from human interests and Calvinism made redemption selective, the Evangelical Revival, deriving its impulse from Luther and the Moravians, proclaimed the universality of divine grace for all men. All men were objects of redeeming love and therefore redeemable. This universal gospel induced a search for the very lowliest of human beings to whom it applied. The note of universality was struck in the hymns of the Revival, and sounded in the very first it produced, known as the Wesleys' Conversion Hymn:

> Outcasts of men, to you I call,
>   Harlots, and publicans and thieves!
> He spreads His arms to embrace you all.

The very first to be touched by the Revival, it is well known, were the rough, ill-kempt, socially despised miners of Kingswood, Bristol.

As a direct result of the Evangelical Revival a whole range of new social sympathies was evoked: ministries to the poor, visitation of prisons, provision of schools, a challenge to slavery. Not that the results of the Revival were all as unequivocal as this. The admitted toryism of Wesley frowned on political revolution. Some of his followers shared his outlook, but the gospel he preached gave birth to democratic convictions in others. The great bulk of the Methodist communities which sprang up as a result of the Revival were composed of working people, miners in coal, iron and tin, cotton and woollen weavers and agricultural labourers. The very gospel which had transformed life for them and given new meaning to their existence gave birth to new impulses of liberty, a new self-respect, and promptings for the betterment of their earthly lot. The beginnings of British Trade Unionism owe something to these impulses and promptings derived from the Great Revival, as the testimony of the Webbs in their *History of Trade Unionism* bears witness. Six of the seven Tolpuddle Martyrs were Methodist Local Preachers, and Primitive Methodists in Durham and East Anglia were leaders in the struggle for improvement in the conditions of mining and agricultural life.

The wider impact of the Evangelical Revival can be traced the world over, again in a reaching out to the lowliest and a raising of the standard of the common man's life wherever the Gospel has been allowed to do its work freely. The eighteenth and nineteenth centuries saw an extension of the horizons of life not incomparable with that of the sixteenth. The eighteenth century intensified the colonization of America and brought Australia and the Pacific Islands within our ken, and the nineteenth century saw the opening up of Africa. Each fresh development, as Latourette shows, brought new incentives for the spread of the Christian religion. Christianity kept pace with the advancing frontiers of American civilization, and religion went wherever the settlers went. A Northamptonshire shoemaker was fired by reading the *Journals* of Captain Cook, and concern for the cannibals of the South Seas became a flame. Christian Missions have sometimes been caricatured as mere expeditions in proselytism and intolerable interference with other religions. They can, however, justify themselves—if justification be needed—by a multitude of ministries to human need and uplifting. The first Methodist Missions, for example, were to West Indian slaves, and the archives of both the Methodist and Baptist Societies show how their agents participated in the struggle for emancipation. In the South Seas, communities of people in Samoa, Fiji and New Guinea, once the home of cannibalism, bear testimony to the morally transforming powers of religion. Medical and educational missionary work in China and India have also communicated transforming influences to Chinese peasantry, Miao aboriginals in Yunnan, and the "untouchable" outcaste classes of India. Some quite unmistakable political reactions ensued. A new democratic Chinese nationalism owed something to Christian teaching, and the Christian community in India, mostly outcaste, has won recognition as a political minority. In Africa, a chain of institutions from Lovedale in South Africa and Blantyre in Livingstonia to Achimota on the Gold Coast, tell of efforts, continually readjusted to meet the lessons of experience, to help the African to find himself. On the copper belt in the Rhodesias, concern for the African uprooted from his tribal life and exposed to the exploitations and demoralizations of Western industrialism is a foremost activity of the Christian missionary. Uganda, in the very heart of the continent, is a further witness to the transformations in social life which Christianity can produce. Christian faith, therefore, must be counted among the agencies concerned for the redemption of the common man.

III

THE EMERGENCE OF THE COMMON MAN

IN THE YEAR 1942, just after his country had entered the second World War, Mr. Henry A. Wallace, then Vice-President of the U.S.A., let fall a phrase that may well become historic: "The century on which we are entering—the century that will come out of this war—can be and must be the century of the common man."

I

How far can such judgment be sustained? Has "the common man" really emerged, and if so, in what sense?

Two remarkable facts confront us. The first is that, to an extent unprecedented in human history, political power has come to him. In the most highly developed modern nation states citizenship has steadily extended to the whole adult population. The electoral franchise in Britain, for example, which prior to the Reform Bill of 1832 was possessed by less than half a million out of a population of 20,000,000, is since the Franchise Act of 1918 now possessed by all adult persons, men and women, above the age of twenty-one, numbering over 34,000,000 persons of all classes out of a population of 46,000,000. A Presidential Election in the U.S.A. will enlist the suffrages of nearly 50,000,000 American citizens. Twenty-two million votes were cast in the Italian election which decided the fate of the Italian monarchy, and the French electorate numbers nearly 20,000,000. A small country like Greece, with a population of 4,000,000 has an electoral roll of nearly of 2,000,000.

The spread of parliamentary institutions and the creation of mass electorates are outstanding political phenomena of our time. The opinion of the common man counts in the world of politics. By his collective decisions he can and does make and unmake governments, and to this extent at least modern democracies have their destinies in their own hands.

There is, however, a new portent in the democratic sky. So far the parliamentary institutions reviewed rest mainly on the basis of two-party systems and majority rule. The U.S.S.R. presents us with the democratic phenomenon of a one-party system and minority rule, and in the name of democracy not only upholds its conception in the vast domains under its control that now stretch from the Vistula to the Pacific, but also seeks to commend it to, if not enforce it upon, other peoples, particularly in Eastern Europe, under its influence. Moreover, in lands and amongst peoples where the older democratic conception is still dominant, there are active supporters of the Soviet system who would wish to see it enacted elsewhere.

Is the rise of the Soviet system, then, another sign of the emergence of the common man? This much seems relevant. The system emerged from a Revolution directly designed to bring the common man into his own, and its initial success was due to the appeal to soviets or councils of workers, soldiers and sailors, and to the land hunger of the Russian peasant. It was in fact a " proletarian " revolution remarkable for its opportunism, skilfully led by a small group of resolute men, whose professed aim was the deliverance of the common man in Russia from—absolute monarchial rule and economic exploitation. To the Soviet system, indeed, is given the specious description: " Dictatorship of the Proletariat." The phrase, however, is ambiguous. Its meaning in practice is: Party Dictatorship on behalf of the Proletariat. The real rulers in the U.S.S.R. are a small group of able and determined men, of very doctrinaire habit of mind, sustained by a minority party, carefully selected and strictly disciplined, whose will, once declared, is law. This dictatorship is said to be necessary until the proletariat in whose interests it works is equipped and trained for corporate communal life. Then the State will wither and the classless and stateless community at last be realized. Meanwhile the acts of dictatorship are covered by a democratic façade. While citizenship in the early days of the Revolution was strictly limited to workers, the Soviet constitution of 1936 created an electoral system by which the franchise, on the one party model, was extended to all over eighteen, irrespective of race, colour or creed. An election in Russia on the new style brings to the poll a mass electorate numbering 100,000,000, and when the complicated system of soviets, local, national and international is remembered, it is possible that the voice of the common man is heard more than the world outside knows. But any confident word about the Russian system has still to be spoken. The most we can say, speaking from the outside, is that it is avowedly the common man who is in view, and so far, in Russia also he has emerged.

II

This acquisition of political power by the common man has been accompanied by a social revolution, sometimes gradual, sometimes swift and cataclysmic, which has given a new shape and contour to social life. One evidence of it is the diminished power of arbitrary kingship in the world. Absolute monarchies have disappeared from view in China and Russia; imperial thrones have crashed in Germany and Austria, regions once the home of countless petty principalities; kings have gone into exile from Belgium, Italy, Spain and Yugoslavia; exiled and brought back by the people's will in Greece. So far as absolutism survives among the princes of India, it is probably not likely long so to continue. The Turkish sultanate has been abolished, and where kingship still persists in the East as in Persia and Egypt, it is allied with parliamentary government. Only in the lands of N.W. Europe and in Great Britain does monarchy still continue on a relatively stable foundation, and there it is when dynasties are firmly established, for historic reasons, in the affections of the people, when kings are democrats and the powers of monarchy are strictly limited. Elsewhere over vast areas the tendency is to republican forms of government, government of the people, by the people and for the people, to use again the historic phrase of President Lincoln. The one qualification is that when and where democratic institutions break down, the tendency, as Plato long ago affirmed from experience must be the case, is for dictatorship or tyranny to appear on its ruins.

Aristocracy based on birth and hereditary ownership of land is being eliminated from the earth almost more rapidly than kingship. It has been more ruthlessly extirpated in the U.S.S.R.; there are no more barons in Russia. Nor are junkers likely to be seen again in East Prussia and the surviving French or Italian nobilities are pale shadows of their former greatness. Everywhere the last traces of feudal ownership of the land steadily disappear; great estates become collective farms in Russia, or are broken up among peasant proprietors in France or sold to tenant farmers, as in Britain, when they are not transformed into limited liability companies or made over as gifts to the National Trust. One may conceive that in Japan the feudalism that survived has received a blow from which it will not recover.

Change, too, is upon the residual capitalist middle-class of industrialists, merchants and manufacturers, whose power, won by struggle from the landed aristocracy, is now in turn challenged by the power of the people en masse. In the U.S.S.R., the entire class of rich bourgeoisie, to use Marx's ungainly phrase, has been expropriated down to the more prosperous farmers, and the means of production, except for small one-man industries, taken over by the State. Heavy taxation in Britain has almost liquidated the very rich, as well as broken up the great landed estates, and the disparities between wealth and poverty are reduced. Similar tensions are discernible in every organized industrial nation, with resultant tendencies for the State more and more to plan, control and take over the means of production in the interests of the people. Even in the U.S.A., the home of big business and unrepentant individualism, the first faint signs of writing on the wall begin to appear, accompanied by the rumblings of organized labour and the portent of state action in the economic realm. The one qualification is the striking emergence of a new middle class, or perhaps we may say ruling class, or aristocracy, composed of scientists, technicians and industrial managers, in what James Burnham calls "the managerial revolution".

Meanwhile from the ranks of the common man, men of strength of character, capacity and will, have found a way to positions of responsibility in government once reserved for the privileged few. Mid-nineteenth-century America used to glow with pride in the career of Abraham Lincoln, who passed from log cabin to White House. But in our day, even before Mr. Ernest Bevin, we have seen a working engineer, who once ran bare-footed in the streets of Newcastle, become Foreign Secretary of Great Britain and chosen, though with fateful results for him, to preside over an international assembly of representatives of the nations. Joseph Stalin, the leading figure in the U.S.S.R., is a man of the people, of the humblest origins, and so was Sun Yat Sen in China, and the same might be said of many another personality in the world political scene. Labour Governments begin to be the order of the day in many lands.

What most concerns us, however, is the change in the actual condition of the common man. His material well-being is the conscious aim of government throughout the world to an extent probably undreamed of in any previous age. In part it is a response to the claims of social justice and a recognition of the common man's right to an equitable

C

share in the material goods of life. In part also it is the reward of his own unremitting struggle for more reasonable conditions of life and labour and a first-fruit of his achievement of political power. He has staked his claim to a more equal distribution of opportunity and material good. So the development of the social services goes on apace to lift the burden of economic poverty from the shoulders of the common man and his family, to guard him against indigence, sickness, idleness and ignorance. The modern State now counts it an obligation to provide him with a house in which to make a home for himself and his family, with help to maintenance and increasing educational opportunities by which they can be better equipped for the race of life. This is the avowed intention of the new era in Russia: for a still longer period it has been the increasing aim of government in Britain and other countries of Western Europe. The lifting of the material standard of life for the common man is an objective of a vast amount of social effort and political action the world over; and the common man appears to be coming into his own. What he will do with it has yet to be proven.

IV

THE STRUGGLE FOR THE COMMON MAN'S SOUL

(1) *Irreligion*

THE AFFIRMATION is frequently made that as the common man has come into his own, the influence of religion on him has receded. He has, it is said, in countless cases ceased to feel any need of it, or to deem that it has any relevance to his life. Often enough, when questioned on the matter he reveals colossal ignorance about it, and so far as he has any interest in it, his mind is a jumble of confused, diverse and contradictory ideas. So much is clear from reviews of popular opinion like that set out in the Mass Observation Study: *Puzzled People*, or the more penetrating studies of E. G. Lee in *Mass Man and Religion*, or Dr. C. P. Martin in *The Decline of Religion*.

The causes of this are manifold. Part of the reason is the natural man's apathy in regard to fundamental questions as to the why and wherefore of his existence. Faith is not easy to him. A great deal is due to the fret of the common man's reaction to the bitter economic struggle: anxiety about daily bread and preoccupation with the getting of it may dull his finer sensibilities. On the top of this has come his obsession with the struggle for political power: politics have become a substitute for religion. To say this is not to deny the validity of his interest in the political struggle as a means of achieving justice: it is to say that the domination of the political interest is in part illusory, and the complete remedy for his dire extremity is not to be found along that road. But what in this chapter we are mainly concerned with is something beyond all this. It is that the forces of religion and irreligion have been beating about his head and struggling for possession of his spirit. With this struggle we must now reckon.

I

In this conflict of religion and irreligion the situation of the common man is part of the situation of European man in general. The revolt from religion has become a marked feature of the Western world. The springs of rebellion can be traced as far back as the Renaissance and the Reformation, though we can discern signs of it long before those epoch-making upheavals. The Reformation repudiated authority which interposed itself between man and God, and the Renaissance as emphatically rejected authority's claim to set limits to the search for factual truth or to finality about ultimate questions of human existence.

Both movements had significance for the common man. The one set him free in his judgment and his conscience, and allowed him to read and interpret the Word of God for himself as the Spirit of truth enlightened him. The other, as soon as its influence began to penetrate his mind, helped him to understand and master the material conditions of mundane existence without reference to the ultimate supernatural ground of that existence, or any unproven world of the hereafter.

Both movements thus had a sceptical edge, calculated to influence the common man's attitude to religion. The Reformation, asserting the freedom of his conscience and his right to judge for himself, carried with it liberty to deny as well as to affirm, to reject as well as to accept. The Renaissance, so far as it was preoccupied with man and external nature, ultimately left little room for thoughts of God or immortality. The Reformation, however, did hold man to his need of God by reason of his sinful nature, and counteracted the Renaissance tendencies to preoccupation with external nature by its deep sense of the perplexing nature of man himself. It was the tendencies that flowed from the Renaissance that at long last, uniting with the common man's rebellion against his material lot and the social injustice from which he suffered, helped to turn his mind against religion.

II

Only the merest outline of the stages of this revolt against religion can be indicated here.

We take, for example, the influence of the English Deists and their followers the French Encyclopædists as they ultimately reacted upon the French Revolution. The Deists would not, it is true, have thought of themselves as the servants of irreligion, but rather as the exponents of natural religion based upon reason, as opposed to revealed religion. Yet whatever service they may have ultimately rendered to religion or theology by compelling a new apologetic and a new approach to the Bible, much of their influence was negative. Their doctrine of creation made God remote from His world, and therefore more unapproachable by man. Hence prayer and communion lost their reality, and religion was reduced to a faith and a morality resting on individual reason. If the influence of Deism in England was mainly temporary and evanescent, it was not so in its effect, mediated through Voltaire, on French contemporary thought. The Encyclopædists derive their name from their enterprise in compiling an encyclopædia of the new scientific knowledge that was crowding in on the world. They were a group of scientific thinkers—the names of Diderot, D'Alembert, Holbach and Helvetius figure among them—who were the inheritors of the scientific revolution which followed the work of Kepler and Copernicus, Francis Bacon and Galileo, Pascal and Newton.

The universe was conceived more and more as a self-contained system, moving by its own energies and directed by its own laws. The hypothesis of God as its Creator and Prime Mover and always necessary to its existence seemed less and less requisite to men more and more preoccupied with secondary causes. It was the connection between events, rather than the why and wherefore of them, that engaged their attention and excited their wonder. To seek to understand the order of the material universe and to bring it to bear upon the disorder of human society seemed a way of deliverance upon which it was quite possible to dispense with religion. Not that the Encyclopædists were agreed upon this. Some like D'Alembert, Helvetius and Holbach, were sceptics and atheists. Others, like Voltaire, remained Deists. But through much of the Encyclopædia ran hostility to religion in general and Christianity in particular.

When, however, this tendency was related to social and political conditions in eighteenth-century France, its sceptical and revolutionary force was heightened. " A dissolute court and a despotic government, on the one hand, and a Church both hypocritical and tyrannical, on the other, had, each in its respective sphere, alienated not only the poor and suffering, but all thinking men. . . . The impulse on their part was to resist the tyranny and corruption that everywhere abounded."[1] So it was that in the Revolution, not only was the monarchy overthrown, but religion was discarded. What use had the proletariat of the Faubourg St. Antoine for religion?

A not dissimilar situation emerged in Britain. The trend of thought was typified, almost as by no other, by Tom Paine, the influence of whose *Rights of Man* on radical politics in Britain has already been noticed. No less remarkable was the effect of his later work, *The Age of Reason*. There is something dramatic in the way in which, under imminent peril of arrest towards the end of the Reign of Terror in which culminated the Revolution he had so

[1] *Encyclopaedia of Religion and Ethics*, Vol. V, pp. 302-3.

eloquently defended, he hurried to give effect to his long-deferred intention to publish before he died his thoughts on religion. His intention was precipitated and his work made necessary, he declared, by "the circumstance that has taken place in France of the total abolition of the priesthood and of everything appertaining to compulsive systems of religion and compulsive articles of faith". He is concerned lest in the general wreck of superstition, of false systems of government and false theology, true morality, humanity and theology may be lost sight of. He roundly affirmed his deistic faith:

> I believe in one God and no more, and I hope for happiness beyond this life.
> I believe in the equality of man; and I believe that religious duties consist in doing justice, loving mercy and endeavouring to make our fellow-creatures happy.

His negations were equally emphatic:

> I do not believe in the creed professed by the Jewish Church, by the Roman Church, by the Greek Church, by the Turkish Church, by the Protestant Church, nor by any church that I know of. My own mind is my own Church.

The negative side of Paine's creed had probably more effect than the positive. He developed with it a bitter, almost vitriolic attack on the Christian Creed and the Christian Scriptures. While he expressed approbation of the character of Jesus of Nazareth as an amiable philanthropist, he rudely dismissed the whole structure of faith built upon that slender history, "the strange fable of the Christian Creed", as constructed by its propagators for mercenary ends.

The influence of Paine's writings upon the working-class mind of Britain was strong in his own day and the following generation, and has persisted in a diffused way until our own time. *The Rights of Man* became a text-book for

radical reformers, and when they had read it, they turned to
The Age of Reason, and reforming zeal become indoctri-
nated with unbelief in revealed religion. Of Francis Place,
the Radical Tailor of Charing Cross, we are told that *The
Age of Reason* shattered his Christianity, and so far from
finding repose in Deism, he became an out-and-out atheist,
and made no secret of his disbelief in God. The sensational
circumstances of the publication of *The Rights of Man* led
to a phenomenal circulation, it is said, of a million and a half
copies in Britain alone. From now on, in the minds of
many, the struggle for political reform and social justice was
associated with the denial of revealed religion and with
irreligion. Later in the same succession comes Charles Brad-
laugh, the confessed atheist and secularist, and, nearer our
own time, after the reading of Hæckel's *Riddle of the
Universe*, Robert Blatchford, of *Clarion* fame.

III

While enmity to religion pervaded large tracts of radical
and revolutionary thought in Europe during the whole of
the nineteenth century, a more relentless and more persistent
hostility broke in on the world with the emergence of
atheistic Marxian Communism. Marx and Engels both
had some familiarity with religion. Marx belonged to a
Jewish family with a rabbinical background, which had
become conventionally Christian. Engels was reared in the
Protestant tradition. Why, then, did their espousal of the
plight of the European proletariat carry them to so complete
a repudiation of religion?

The reason, it would seem, had little to do directly with
the proletariat whose cause they espoused. It was a
philosophical revolt, a revolution in the world of ideas,
which they brought to the interpretation of the revolutionary
fervour which had taken possession of them. The clue is
supplied by Engels himself in a tiny monograph, published
as late as 1888, entitled: *Feuerbach, the Roots of the Socialist*

Philosophy. Engels' starting-point is the period of preparation for the German Revolution of 1848. In Germany then, as in France in the eighteenth century, revolutionary philosophic conceptions brought about a break-up of existing political conditions. The philosophic revolt was directed against the great Hegel, whose conception of the State had become a royal Prussian philosophy of government, a philosophical benediction of despotism, police government, star-chamber justice and censorship. It was so understood by Frederick William III and his subjects. The State of Prussia was the embodiment of Absolute Spirit.

Revolt against this came from some of Hegel's own pupils, and became open and avowed when in 1840 orthodox pietism and absolutist feudal reaction ascended the throne with Frederick IV. To deny the dominant religion and the existing State became the first objective of the rebels. Because politics, wrote Engels, were at that time a very thorny field, the main fight was directed against religion. Supernatural religion was repudiated along with Hegel's philosophic groundwork for it in the Absolute. But if Absolute Spirit was no longer the basis of reality, what was? Refuge could only be found in a materialistic conception of Nature itself, and resort to this was made possible by the work of Feuerbach. Hence the title of Engels' monograph. Feuerbach's work in *The Essence of Christianity* and *The Essence of Religion*, says Engels, " placed Materialism on the throne again without any intervention. Nature exists independently of all philosophies. It is the foundation on which we, ourselves products of nature, are built. Outside man and nature nothing exists, and the higher beings which our religious fantasies have created are only the fantastic reflections of our individuality." On such a view, supernatural religion could be repudiated, and recourse made easy to atheism—denial that the idea of God was necessary to explain nature—and to the philosophy of materialism.

The full force of this atheistic materialism was not felt, however, until it was applied, as it was so ruthlessly and vigorously by Marx, to human life and history. It then turned dialectical materialism—the process in nature—into historical materialism or the materialist conception of history. As men's tools change, so society changes. But the change is revolutionary and catastrophic, because it turns on struggle for the means of production. "The history of all human society, past and present," wrote Marx and Engels in the well-known words of the Communist Manifesto of 1848, "has been the history of class struggles." This history had now culminated in the struggle between bourgeois and proletariat, brought about by capitalist ownership of the means of production, where labour and machines were ruthlessly exploited for gain. The issue of the struggle could only be in violent revolution, the seizure of the means of production, factories and land, by the proletariat, the creation of classless society based on equality of work and supply of need, and the ultimate withering away of the State.

At this point, this involved and abstruse dialectical philosophy could become intelligible to the common man, and kindle his revolutionary zeal. Deterministic though the philosophy claimed to be, here was a revolution in which he could be urged to join with all the force of his being. Why he should need to be urged to join it when history was carrying him that way of itself is not so clear. When, to advance the revolution, he was warned to be on his guard against religion, atheism then seemed to be both natural and necessary. It was Marx who coined the phrase: "Religion is the opium of the people", which was to be one of the slogans of the Communist Movement.

How deeply embedded in the whole Marxian movement is this hostility to religion is seen when, finally, we glance at Lenin's opinions on the subject. These are set out in a small volume in the *Little Lenin Library*, entitled: *Lenin on Religion*. We summarize three short paragraphs from an article in *Novaya Zhin*, December, 1905, there quoted: "Religion," declares Lenin, "is a form of spiritual oppression weighing upon the exploited masses, crushed by continuous toil, poverty and deprivation. Their helplessness inevitably generates belief in a better life after death, as the helplessness of the savage in his primitive struggle with nature gave rise to belief in gods and devils. Religion teaches the toiling poor to be resigned and patient in this world, consoling them with the hope of reward in heaven. Religion also teaches those who live by the labour of others to be 'charitable', in order to justify their exploitation of others, and provide them with 'a cheap ticket to heaven'. 'Religion is the opium of the people', a kind of spiritual intoxicant, drowning their humanity and blunting their desire for a decent human existence. The class-conscious worker of to-day, brought up in the environment of a big factory," Lenin goes on, "rejects religious prejudices with contempt, leaving heaven to priests and bourgeois hypocrites. He fights for a better life for himself, here on earth, ranging himself on the side of Socialism, which, with the help of science, is dispersing the fog of religion, liberating workers from faith in life after death, and rallying them to present-day struggle for better existence here and now."

These terse sentences are in Lenin's own words. Whether they are universally true of the world's workers is open to doubt. They are true of many. They are also what atheistic Marxian Communism desires to be true and thinks should be true. As the teachings of Marx, Engels and Lenin penetrate the working-class mind or capture some credulous members of the scientific intelligentsia they are judgments in which many men come to believe.

V

THE STRUGGLE FOR THE
COMMON MAN'S SOUL

(2) *The Voices of Religion*

AT THE SAME TIME that irreligion, in a chorus of strident voices, has sought to captivate the common man, the age-long struggle of religion for his soul has gone on. To that side of the struggle we now turn. What is the nature of the hold that religion has sought to win over him?

I

There is an initial difficulty. Religion speaks with many voices, and its utterances, like those of irreligion, diverge in a bewildering way. Whatever be the primary impulse of the human spirit which brings religion forth, its issues are amazing in their fecundity and variety, from primitive *mana* and *tabu* up to the rationalized religion of a civilized man. Myth and legend abound, and superstition may lurk in the oddest corners to preserve many an ungrounded belief. We need only note the contrast between the great religions: Confucianism, Brahmanism, Buddhism, Judaism, Islam and Christianity. Yet each of these makes its appeal to masses of common folk: Chinese and Indian peasantry, children of the Ghetto, peoples of the Arab and Persian worlds, and the European proletariat. When atheistic Communism sets out on its anti-God campaign, it ranges itself against every one of the great religions without distinction.

The record of the Christian religion is scarred with this tale of divergence. History took a fateful turn, for example, when the Eastern Church broke with the Western and the Southern and Russian Slavs took their Christianity from Constantinople and not from Rome. Europe became divided from that hour into Eastern and Western, and when Constantinople fell before the Turks in 1453, the claim was put forward that now Moscow must be the "third Rome" and there can never be another. "Messianism" entered into the soul of the Russian people, and underlies the Russian attitude to the rest of mankind. Russia and her people are now to be the "saviours" of the world.

So we come again to the Reformation, which shattered the Western Church into fragments. When we talk of Christianity in Western Europe, we must speak of Romans, Lutherans, and Calvinists. When we think of Christianity in Britain, we must do so in terms of Anglicans and again Romans and also Baptists, Congregationalists, Methodists, Presbyterians, Friends and the Salvation Army. The diversity is bewildering, and whatever may be the historic grounds and justification for the divisions, they add enormously to the complexity of the problem. In what form of religion shall the common man come to his rest?

II

Yet with all this, an impressive strength of organization still goes to the spread and propagation of religion. It is well to measure critically the instruments of persuasion which are to hand in the service of what is so often rather unhappily called "organized religion". By what means can and do the Churches maintain the appeal of faith? Some years ago, for instance, a continental statistician made an estimate of the numbers of clergy in the service of the Roman and Protestant communions of Europe. The number, small in proportion to the total population, ran into hundreds of thousands. But, he enquired, what ought to be the influence of a specially selected and trained body of men, with unique opportunities of persuasion, around whose calling gathers peculiarly the odour of sanctity, upon the mind of the community as a whole?   And, as our eyes go searching through the earth, we may well wonder as we think of Confucian sages, Brahmanic holy men, Buddhist priests, Moslem mullahs, Jewish rabbis and Christian clergy: what is it in religion that gathers to itself this huge apparatus of persuasion?   The ministry of religion, even though some of the awe that once attended it has gone from it, is still a force to be reckoned with in the common life of men.   The truth of what they declare, and the validity of its influence on human life, is the test question.

Nor is this all.   Behind the minister of religion stands the organized religious community; in Christian parlance, " the Church " or " the Churches ". So history and tradition at once come into play.   A faith like that of the Christian religion with its roots far back in the past, sustained by the memory of great historic events the annual commemoration of which marks the cycling year, and which has survived the vicissitudes of history until now, and manifests continual powers of renewal and adaptation to changing circumstances, is a faith that inevitably challenges attention.   Somehow we feel the spirit of life must be in it.   " I pay tribute to you in history," Lord Morley is reputed to have said to a Roman priest, " though I am afraid of you."   The strength of this tradition of life handed on from age to age and generation to generation is an undoubted ground for appealing for faith.   Behind every worshipping Christian community is a spiritual ancestry that links it with the Upper Room in Jerusalem and the lakeside of Galilee, if indeed it does not go further back and link it in the community of souls with faithful Abraham.   Still further, as devout Christians everywhere would generally testify, in the central act of their worship, be it known as Lord's Supper, Holy Communion or the Mass, they celebrate the great act of God by which their redemption is accomplished, and receive within themselves the renewal of that divine life by which their life and faith are sustained. It is perhaps a moot question, as yet unanswerable, whether the forces of irreligion can create instruments of persuasion, or rear a structure of faith and experience as commanding as those of religion.

We must go further. Over against the central supreme figure in the Christian tradition, the Person of Christ, stands a store of other sacred memories and lesser loyalties. There are saints and martyrs in all ages, the memory of whom is blessed, and " the communion of saints ", the tie that binds the believer here and now with the unnumbered host of all who have lived and died in the Christian faith, is a cherished article of Christian belief. Even the divisions of Christendom, however much the fact of them is to be regretted, add to the store of holy memories and precious loyalties. We recall what the name of St. Sergius means to the devout soul in Russia, or what that of St. Francis of Assisi has meant to all Christendom. Every Christian has the work of Origen, Athanasius, or Augustine for part of his heritage. He may draw inspiration, if he will, from the spiritual heroism of a Luther, the penetrating mind of a Calvin, the spiritual insight of a George Fox, the experience in inner travail of a Bunyan, and the apostolic power of a Wesley.

III

The power of a religion to influence the life of the common man derives from this experience of faith, at one and the same time both communal and individual, by which he derives strength from the divine life communicated to him. He sees life in a new perspective: not merely as that of a creature in time, but as an heir of the ages with eternity as his real sphere. From God he comes: to God he returns!

At once the events of his earthly life take on a new significance. His birth becomes in some sense a divine event. When he finds a chosen mate with whom to make a home, and, of free will on both sides, marries to begin the cycle of life afresh, he is conscious that it is a sacred act, for the perfect fulfilment of which the exceeding grace of God is needed. As he faces the end of his earthly life, he knows no fear or regret, for he believes in " the forgiveness of sins, the resurrection of the body and the life everlasting ", and he knows he goes home to God! The transfiguring power of religion is seen not least in its power to take common facts of life, birth, mating and death, and wreathe around them divine meaning which lifts them into the light of immortality.

At this point the strident challenge of irreligion is once more heard. How does your religion, thus conceived, touch the common man's material lot, the earning of his daily bread, the government of his community, his economics, his politics and his communal life? With those questions in detail a large part of the rest of this book will attempt directly to deal. Here it is enough to say that in the experience of those of the ranks of the common man who share the Christian faith and life it has everything to do! For when all is said and done, the great majority of Christian people everywhere are drawn from the common people. It has always been so. Many of the early Christians were drawn from the ghettoes and slave populations of Graeco-Roman cities. " Not many wise . . . not many mighty, not many noble, are called: but God chose foolish things . . . weak things . . . and the things that are despised," was St. Paul's boast to his first converts at Corinth. It has been the same in all succeeding ages, even when Christianity has attracted to itself the patronage of the great and mighty. In Britain to-day it might be affirmed that the majority of people in the Churches are working people. It ought to be so, because there are more working people than any other kind. The proof will be found in Churches in rural and industrial areas: they will be found to be manned largely by farmers, farm labourers, miners, weavers, fishermen, potters, steel-workers, engine-drivers and so on.

This does not mean that the Christian Church is a class

community, though Christian congregations take on the character of the classes from which their adherents are drawn, and there are well-to-do congregations, and middle-class congregations as well as working-class ones. The Christian Church ideally is a community in which people of all classes meet on equal terms, where there is neither bond nor free, but all are one in Christ Jesus. The appeal of religion is to all classes: well-to-do, professional, intelligentsia, artisan and hand-worker—for their need of religion is common to all. Yet, if it is a question of religion and the common man, then the majority of the people in the Churches are working folk. Not by any means the majority of their class: but the majority of Christians! And if you test their lives, their judgments and their reactions to affairs, you will find how much their work and their politics are coloured by their religion.

IV

One more critical consideration, however, has to be taken into account. What of the impact of the Christian community on society as a whole? In the attack on religion, some of the bitterest criticism is directed, not against Christians as such, but against the communities of Christians, the Churches. They are, we are told, strongholds of re-action, enemies of progress, hives of superstition, impervious to new knowledge, unable to withstand the light of truth. So we have the strange paradox: from within, to those who know and revere her, the Church is sacred and holy, a creation of loveliness, the Bride of Christ. From without, she appears an object of scorn, ridicule and contempt. That the Christian Church should be an object of criticism and an occasion of offence is no new thing. It has been so from the beginning. In the first centuries of its history in the Roman Empire it was often accounted a treasonable society. The Middle Ages were fraught with the strife of Church and Empire, and in the end the medieval Church was rejected

D

by a great portion of Western Europe as an evil and corrupt thing. The repudiation of papacy as anti-Christ and the sweeping away of monastic institutions are events at which still to marvel.

What here concerns us is the insistent criticism of their attitude to the material lot of the common man. It is the gravamen of the Marxist criticism of religion, that it is the opium of the people, dulling their sense of present wrongs by the promise of better life hereafter. In books telling the grim story of the Industrial Revolution in Britain, such as those of the Hammonds—*The Town, Skilled and Village Labourers*—or Cole and Postgate—*The Common People, 1796-1946* the comment is often bitter—that pious philanthropy had no remedy but charity for the wrongs of the poor : while the voice of the Churches was seldom lifted in their behalf, except to counsel patient submission to their lot.

There is unmistakable evidence to sustain this judgment, evidence every recital of which leaves us sore and wondering. Nothing is gained by seeking to mitigate it. Yet the full story is not so absolutely one-sided as is sometimes suggested. There is evidence which points in the other direction to deepening concern and passionate endeavour. There is, for example, the judgment of Peter Drucker in his book, *The End of Economic Man*, that in the nineteenth century the most radical criticism of free capitalist society came, not from Marxianism, but from the Christian side : " The history of the hundred years before the World War (1914-18) is usually seen as the history of the growth and development of *bourgeois* capitalism and of its Siamese twin and antagonist Marxian Socialism. Yet it can be also interpreted as the history of the emergence of Christian criticism of the mechanical and economic concept of society, and of the increasing awareness in the Churches that, and why, this concept must fail." French Catholic thinkers— was he thinking of Lammenais?—first argued, he declares, that capitalism would necessarily destroy itself by creating class war, German Christian conservatives that class war could only lead to greater inequality and despair, to end finally, according to a Spanish Catholic, in the self-destruction of civilization. Drucker goes further, and pays tribute to the success of the Christian attempts, on the Continent and in Britain, to provide a basis for a new non-mechanist society. The great majority of the institutions of present-day society, he declares, which make life tolerable for the masses owe their origins to these religious forces, because they are not built upon the collapsed concept of Economic Man. He quotes the work of Shaftesbury in the British Factory Acts, of German Evangelicals in introducing social insurance, and of Quaker industrialists in advocating decent working conditions, a living wage and protection against accidents. He might have gone further still, and noted the effect on Continental Labour of the famous Encyclical of Pope Leo XIII: *The Condition of the Working Classes*, the influence of successive *Social Creeds* of the Federal Council of the Churches of Christ on public opinion and government action in the U.S.A., and the effect on the attitude of the Christian Churches in Britain to social change produced by the Copec Conference of 1924 and its successors.

Nevertheless, it is still necessary to turn a discerning and critical eye on the corporate influence of the Churches on the communities amid which they work. If we briefly survey the record of the Church of Rome and the great Protestant Communions since the Reformation, a mottled picture emerges. Churches, like all other institutions of which human nature is the raw material, are, so far, but " earthen vessels " which may conceal, rather than unveil, the divine " treasure " of which they are the guardians. Lust of power, the instinct of self-preservation, undue subservience to temporal authority, may pollute their spirit and warp their influence. Decline in faith and spiritual insight may come upon them: " the world " may enter and contaminate. Bigotry and fanaticism may flourish like foul diseases. The sinister influence of the Jesuit Order on the

France of Louis XIV or the England of James II is a case in point. Or we may consider the changing spiritual tempo of religious life in the Church of England since the Reformation, as it has lived through the age of Puritanism, the High Church Revival, the somnolence of the eighteenth century, and refreshing signs of spiritual awakening in the nineteenth and twentieth centuries. Has not English Nonconformity gone through similar periods of rising and waning power?

It is hardest, perhaps, to state the truth about the corporate influence of Roman Catholicism, still probably the strongest single religious force on the Continent of Europe. Despite the apostasy of many of her adherents, her ability to win and retain the love and devotion of her faithful children is a thing to marvel at. But her monarchial form of church government, her feudal outlook and hostility to democracy have often made her an enemy of social progress and political reform. Her intolerant and exclusive claims have made her a foe to liberty, and her ecclesiastical pretensions are a strain on faith. Despite her rigid and closely knit doctrinal formulations, superstition easily lurks within her borders. Her vast resources in wealth seem often gathered by keeping her people very poor, a poverty which her ministries of charity only relieve but do not remove. If we think of Spain and Italy, Ireland or Austria, or the countries of Latin America, it does not appear that Roman Catholic dominated peoples are in the van of human progress.

In Protestantism since the Reformation, the outstanding fact has been the emergence of " national churches " by law established. This transpired in England and Scotland, in Germany and Scandinavia. This was partly the result of a desire to identify the nation with the Christian religion, and to make the Church a prop and mainstay of the existing government. It reversed the medieval position in which the universal Church, the spiritual power, claimed supremacy over the Empire, the temporal power. It brought with it the dubious gains which establishment by the political power gave to the Church: and tended to weaken the Church's independence by turning it into what often seemed a department of state. This was perhaps truer of the Protestant Churches in Germany, and it is not without significance that when Peter the Great introduced his new constitution for the Orthodox Church in Russia, it was on the Prussian model that he framed it, with very fateful consequences for that great communion.

Dire consequences have flowed from this subordination, as it often actually was, of Church to State. It led, for instance, to state efforts to enforce religious uniformity in the interests of national unity, and thereby provoked conscience to revolt. Whenever the Church endeavoured to assert its spiritual liberty, or claimed authority for its own form of government against the popular will, it induced conflicts between Church and State. Perhaps worst of all was the tendency of established churches to lend the weight of their influence to the existing order of government when the forces of political freedom were seeking to reform and liberalize the instrument of government! We have already observed that it was this trend in the Prussian Church in the eighteen-forties which excited the revolutionary hostility of Karl Marx and Frederick Engels.

In distinction to " established churches ", we have also to remark the rise of " free churches ", free, that is, in their right to govern themselves according to conscience without the authority of the State. For long, their right to exist was challenged by authority, and the winning of the right is amongst the most cherished achievements of liberty and democracy. The exercise of this right and liberty of self-government is not, however, without its limitations. It can easily tend to religious arbitrariness and, indeed, anarchy, and to endless division and strife. Moreover, if free from state control, " free churches " have sometimes fallen into the equally perilous control of wealth, and become the tools and instruments of the wealthy trading classes.

What are the lessons to be learned from this long and

complex history of struggle to achieve right relations between Church and State, and to enable the Church to exert its proper influence in the community without fear or let? Clearly, too close an alliance between the Church and the political power has perils for both Church and State. The Church at least must have spiritual autonomy and freedom of prophecy. She must be equally detached from class interest, and free to serve the whole community, and especially the oppressed and under privileged. Often her greatest achievements have been won by prophetic voices from within her own borders, who fearlessly proclaimed the message of her gospel in the behalf of those who most needed it, without fear of restraint or seeking of favour.

VI

THE WORD OF CHRISTIAN FAITH TO THE COMMON MAN

WHAT, out of this medley of voices, and despite the record of strife, division and failure which have marred Christian history, has Christian faith to say to the common man? Beyond the conflict of religion and irreligion, is there a genuine, prophetic and unmistakable word which religion can utter with resounding power in his ear?

I

Much depends on the approach we make to religion. We may start from the human end, with needs and aspirations within us which only God can satisfy. This approach, however, is apt to be deceptive. What we describe as man's search for God is often no more than a desperate desire to hide from Him under the shadow of our uncertainties and self-deceptions. We are afraid of what the vision of God, if we were admitted to behold it, would demand of us. On any view that man is merely a creature of nature the search is no more than wishful thinking, with no assurance of a reality that corresponds with either need or aspiration.

The alternative is to come to the consideration of religion from the Godward end, and follow the way of revelation. Can we ever hope to know God, come to the realization of His presence, or behold the unspeakable vision unless He Himself draws back the veil that hides Him from us and graciously makes Himself known to us? Even here uncertainty may dog us, and our minds and hearts be bemused and befogged by sham revelations and false prophets. We have to test the spirits, whether they really be of God. Yet unless in some way we can be sure that God has indeed spoken from out the unseen world and sought to make Himself known to us, what hope have we of more than a mere earth-bound and transient existence, without enduring meaning or purpose?

What religion has to say to the common man, therefore, must first concern God. Yet even here, it is a question of the common man's capacity to hear what God the Lord doth speak. The natural man may be deaf to the divine voice, and blind to the heavenly vision which is seeking to break upon him. In our day, any word of God to the common man, in addition to overcoming his natural torpor, must break through his obsessions and illusions. He is obsessed by his economic struggle and uncertainty; and has been embittered by the social injustice and wrong from which he has suffered. Any word of God must at least speak to that condition, and show that God is concerned for thwarted justice. Since, however, the cry for justice may be disfigured, especially in days of power and achievement, by cupidity, God's word must be faithful on that score. The common man's illusions are chiefly in the political sphere, eked out by some sense of scientific mastery over natural resource. If he can but dislodge those who have hitherto held power and tyrannized over him, whether politically or economically, he thinks, he himself will, by his own collective power and wit, achieve justice, win freedom and make a paradise of earth. How perilous an illusion it is that by political action he can win his redemption, we shall consider later.

Suppose, however, we can ease his obsessions and lay bare his illusions, then what word of God for him have we? Where and how can we help him to recognize that God has entered into the life of man? The supreme Word of

God upon which the Christian religion has rested all its trust is that God was in Christ, reconciling the world to Himself. It is a thing at which to marvel that the message of Christian redemption should come to the common man in the way it has, mediated through the life of a Palestinian village carpenter, one of " the people of the land ". Humanly speaking, Jesus Christ was Himself a son of the people, who worked with His hands for daily bread. But, as the records show, He so lived, taught, loved, died and rose again, that men who knew Him best deemed Him a visitant from another world, the Divine Redeemer, Son of the Living God, who ushered all who believe in Him into new life. Such is still the verdict of those who know and confide in Him.

Religion's greatest word to the common man, then, is Jesus Christ. What does the common man make of Him? Not everywhere and always does the common man to-day show himself ready to hear or accept the appeal of Christ. The forces of irreligion have inoculated his mind with scepticism and unbelief, and the injustice he has suffered makes him look out on the world with embittered and unbelieving eyes. His distrust of the Church blinds him to the appeal of the Church's Lord. So he may dismiss Christian faith as a fairy tale, not relevant to this rude world. He may imbibe secularist teaching, and indulge in coarse speculations on the manner of Christ's birth. Surrendering to the dogmatism of the dominant atheist and materialist creed, he may recite as it is said the children of Moscow are taught to do: " Christ was a bad man, who deceived the people! "

Yet there are signs that the common man's barriers of resistance can be broken through. Said a German Communist to a Christian pastor who had been proclaiming Christ on the streets of Frankfort, and showing how the Gospel bore on the social problem: " We are afraid of you when you talk that way! You make us think we've to take Christ seriously." On a Lancashire market place a Christian speaker was interrupted by Communist listeners with the question: "Has the Church a programme for society?" "Well, my Church has," he replied. Taking from his pocket a leaflet which set forth some simple objectives for social life framed in terms of justice and freedom, endorsed by his Church, he read it and asked: "Well, what do you think of that?" "A good programme," they said, and then listened to the rest of what he had to say. In the south of England, a Christian minister was invited to speak at a workers' demonstration. He bore his testimony that his life-long social passion was born of his Christian faith and the love of men which the love of Christ inspires. "Won't you get into trouble with your Church for that," the Communist secretary of the demonstration asked. "No," he said, "that's what my Church thinks!" The Communist secretary is now himself a minister of the Christian Church, not the only one who has made a similar pilgrimage back to faith.

We are entitled, therefore, to press the issue upon the common man, and ask him to face it squarely, even in terms of the old question for which there is good Gospel sanction: "What think ye of Christ?" What verdict will he give? The century-old verdict of the Marxists, now echoed so volubly in Moscow? Or will he endorse the testimony of the Christian centuries, verified in the experience of countless millions of believing souls generation after generation? The issue is vital, and the consequences of wrong choice devastating for mankind. Supposing Christ be only a man as we are, and the end of Him be that naked, broken figure on the Cross! Then the materialists are right, and man is only a creature of nature, with no right, justice or love to uphold him, born to live and to die, to crumble to dust and nothingness in the grave, or to be tossed as carrion to the birds of prey. But if it was the Love of God that hung there in the person of Jesus of Nazareth, crucified for us, then our faith is vindicated that we are more than creatures of the dust, that Eternal Righteousness is for ever on the side of the wronged, and that life is stronger than death.

The issue may seem too great to hang upon the nameless death of a Galilean peasant two thousand years ago. Is it really in essence any different from the thousands of nameless deaths of brave youths cut off before their time? The issue is the same. Who are they and what is their ultimate destiny? Even there, as Tennyson showed in his almost forgotten but poignant poem *Rizpah*, there is an irrepressible conviction within us that death is not the end and that love must conquer. But in the case of Jesus Christ, the inner conviction is sustained by the incontrovertible outward evidence of the Resurrection and the faith and experience of the Living Christ, the proven source and guarantee of new life within the heart of the believer. So Christian faith, as set out in its most tremendous expression, is vindicated in experience: " God so loved the world that He gave His only begotten Son, that whosoever believeth in Him, should not perish, but have everlasting life." Is that true? That is the issue the common man must face. He must say!

II

The fact of Christ regarded as the supreme Revelation of God in terms of human life—the Word become flesh—enables us to confront the common man with urgent and fundamental questions concerning the purpose of the universe and the meaning of his existence therein.

Whether the common man ever reflects upon ultimate questions it is hard to say. " Do you know why you were born? " " What is the meaning of life, or the purpose of human existence? " We may put such questions to him, but he will often reply only with a look of blank astonishment. Indeed under the preoccupations of daily life, struggle for bread, experience of frustration and wrong, satisfaction of fleeting desire and weight of crushing sorrow, he may rarely have time to pause and enquire what it is all for. Yet the question may be lingering in the background and some chance encounter bring it into the forefront of consciousness. "I have sometimes wondered that myself," said a working girl for whom life was often grey and dreary, when the question was put in her hearing, "but I never could find the answer."

Popular science and secular philosophies of our day, not unknown to the common man, if only by hearsay and in snippets, make it possible, however, to raise the questions with him. His mentors have made him vaguely acquainted with the smallness of the earth, moving its yearly course in space amid a vast universe of blazing suns and stars, and have told him of the emergence of life on this planet until the earth on land and sea is peopled with a bewildering variety of living species. He will know also, if he has interested himself therein at all, that scientists speculate on the age and history of the earth, and upon the antiquity of man and the possible discontinuance of life when the earth has cooled down, so that living things can no longer exist thereon. In our age, at least, the knowledge of these ideas is widely diffused, and as he follows, however dimly, the story of human life from the cave-man to to-day, the question can be put to the common man with some force: Who is this creature man?

This picture of developing life may lure him, as so many of our generation, on to the false trail of belief in inevitable and necessary progress. Aware of the fact of change, he may be deluded into thinking of it as always change for the better. The peril of disillusionment which this brings is the greater because he is aware of the advances made in our time in the mastery of natural resources. He lives in a world where, in a single generation or so, he has seen men put electricity to daily use, tap waves in the ether and bring the radio to his door, invent the internal combustion engine and the jet aeroplane, split the atom and release cosmic physical powers whose effects for good or ill are well-nigh incalculable.

Aware of all this, the common man is possibly in a mood to listen approvingly to the claims made in the name of science in our day, to be the potential instrument by which man can perfect his environment and regenerate himself. That claim is the chief ground of the facile attraction Marxianism as a doctrine of "scientific socialism" has for credulous members of the scientific intelligentsia and others whom Marxian propaganda has laid under spell. "While the philosophers have sought to *interpret* the universe, the point," as Marx would say, "is to change it." Nor need we grudge them the measure of truth which underlies the contention. Increasing mastery of natural resources and of the elemental powers of the universe should give mankind enlarging control at least of its physical environment. It has done so and may be expected to go on doing so. Developments in biology, such as greater knowledge of the purpose and function of the ductless glands, modification of sex and birth control, may greatly affect living things and bring the possibility of manipulation of human life itself. Human society is to be made a matter of scientific planning, and in the end, we are promised, life on this earth will be perfect and complete!

The common man, however, needs to be reminded that these are in the long run specious and grandiloquent claims. There are humbling questions for him to face. To what end is all this? For what purpose? What is the nature of the being called "man", who is to be subjected to these planned manipulations? From natural laws—whether physical, chemical, biological or psychological—we do not plumb the depths of his being or unveil the mysterious purpose which brought him into the universe. Nor is the universe so friendly to us that we can be sustained in these dreams of progress or mastery. Neither the record of animal species nor the scarred and broken history of man warrants any such optimism. So far as our knowledge goes, the drama of life in the universe is focussed on this planet, but the planet gives us little or no guarantee of being a permanent home for the human race, and none for the individual. Life, in species and individual, comes and goes. Where is the glory that was Greece and the grandeur that was Rome?

With the catastrophes and frustrations of history, past, present and future, in mind, and without a precise and convincing definition of the nature and end of man to guide us, it is not at all clear that scientific planning will ensure us a worth-while life. Our discoveries and inventions may increase our physical convenience, give us light, provide heat and energy more readily and facilitate our mobility, but they will be no more than clever mechanical gadgets, which we may use well or ill. Medical science, our most beneficent science, may bring us far on the way to the banishment of pain and the conquest of disease and prolong life; but death will continue to baffle it. We may, by better agriculture and care of live stock, stave off the peril of hunger that shadows a race that may outgrow its natural resources. Yet, on this basis, it is difficult to see what the final purpose of all our planning and contriving is. The latest aims of biological science, with its talk, not now of eugenics, but of artificial insemination and sex manipulation, to say nothing of euthanasia, seems to offer us little more than the prospect of making the earth a gigantic establishment, akin to a stud farm for race-horses, for the breeding of successive generations of men. What else is the horrifying vision of a book like Mr. Aldous Huxley's *Brave New World*?

Moreover, the whole trend of human history gives little ground for believing in man's achievement of his own perfection, individual or corporate. The mastery which science gives us over natural phenomena is morally neutral; it may be used for good or ill. Civilizations seem to carry the seeds of corruption within themselves, and history is a dismal record of nations that fell, empires that crashed and cultures that have vanished in dust and ruins. The idea of human history as a continuous progress in time moving to a final goal seems far from the truth. It would be more correct to describe it as a movement *across* time. Succeeding generations enter the stream of time, cross it diagonally and pass out on the other side. Then the remorseless questions force themselves upon us: Whence? Why? Whither?

If in some such way, difficult as it may appear to be, we can get the common man to reflect upon the meaning of his existence, we have fresh opportunity to confront him with the significance of Jesus Christ. If He be the Son of God, as Christians believe Him to be, His appearing on this earth is the most significant event in human history. He comes as the revealing Word of God, making plain the meaning of life and the purpose of human existence. In the language of St. Paul, what had been the dark " mystery " hid from the ages now became the " open secret " of the Gospel.[1] The New Testament is radiant with the discovery. Christ is " the way, the truth and the life ". " In him was life, and the life was the light of men." " There was the true light, lighting every man coming into the world." " As many as received him, to them gave he the right to become the children of God, even to them that believe on his name." " Of his fulness we all received, and grace for grace."[2] So life in Christ, the life of the transformed and redeemed children of God in time and eternity, is proclaimed as the goal and purpose of human existence.

In the New Testament again, this unveiling of the divine purpose for human life in Jesus Christ is extended to the whole creation. This may appear astounding to the modern man, accustomed to think of the vastness of the astronomical universe, whether on Einstein's terms or Newton's, or to wonder constantly at the intricacy of living things as revealed by the microscope. The New Testament, however, came to birth in an age which also found the universe vast and mystifying, as the questionings of the Greek philosophers and the fantasies of the Gnostics show.

[1] Eph. 3.1-13.   [2] John 14.6; 1.4, 6, 12, 16.

Did not St. Paul speak of " principalities and powers, and world-rulers of this darkness, and the spiritual hosts of wickedness in high places "?[3] This makes it all the more remarkable that, twice over, the New Testament should affirm that Christ is the key to the understanding of the universe itself. " All things were made by him," says the Fourth Gospel, of Christ as the revealing Word of God, " and without him was not anything made that hath been made."[4] A similar resounding claim is made by St. Paul in the Epistle to the Colossians : " For in him were all things created, in the heavens and upon the earth, things visible and invisible, whether thrones or dominions or principalities or powers; all things have been created through him, and unto him, and he is before all things, and in him all things consist."[5]

Here, then, is something the Christian religion has to say to the common man concerning the meaning of his existence. Wrestling daily with the universe as we do, confronted by its titanic physical powers and emerging life, and perplexed by the mystery of our own being, we may well ask : " What is the purpose of it? " If we trust to our own searching, the problem will baffle us. But for those who have eyes to see, there is light in this one God-given fact, the fact of Jesus Christ. He makes plain the purpose of God in making this world, to make a race of beings conformed to the image of His Son. In the language of an old Christian Father : " Christ became what we are that we might become what He is."[6] And St. Paul, struggling with the problem of a creation that groaned and travailed in pain, spoke of the ultimate hope of all its striving in words that far outstrip our modern conceiving, the hope that " the creation itself shall be delivered from the bondage of corruption into the glorious liberty of the children of God ".[7]

3 Eph. 6.12.   6 Irenaeus: *Adv. Heresios*.
4 John 1.3.   7 Rom. 8.21.
5 Col. 1.16, 17.

III

The appeal of religion to the common man is not alone connected with recognition of the mystery and wonder of the universe; it is also connected more crucially with the mystery of his own nature. Once more we ask: Who is " the common man "? This time the answer is different. He is, if the word of Christian faith be heeded, like everybody else, a being born for communion with the living God, but become sinful, and therefore needing to be " redeemed ".

This view of human nature differs radically from more superficial and optimistic views of it which are current in our time. The Renaissance, as we have observed, and the Age of Enlightenment which followed it, focussed attention on man and his rationality rather than on God. Man was essentially a rational being, able to compass the mystery of his existence and the way of his duty by strength of his unaided reason. One of the governing ideas of William Godwin, dissenting preacher of the eighteenth and nineteenth centuries turned political and religious rebel, in his *Enquiry concerning Political Justice*, we are told, " is to be found in a pathetic belief that men are reasonable beings, that truth when revealed will be recognized as truth, and that men will act accordingly ". That there is an element of rationality in our human make-up is true enough, but we are not wholly so constituted. It is not easy to convince men of the truths of reason or the way of duty, nor even when they admit them to get them to act thereon! There is another side to our nature, the irrational one of instinct and impulse, and as Plato long ago recognized we poor humans are like distracted charioteers, trying to hold the rein on Reason and Desire, two steeds which may pull in opposite directions.

No greater light is to be found in Rousseau's idea of " life according to nature ", which decried the artificialities and unrealities of civilization and exalted " the noble

E

savage " and the native reactions of the child-mind. Out of this came an educational theory which has the merit of making instructors of youth pay more attention to the nature of the human material on which they have to work, but has given birth to indiscipline under the guise of free self-expression of untutored impulse, a result not so meritorious. It is here we find the ground of a notion often loudly proclaimed of " the essential goodness of human nature ", a notion which is strangely belied by the facts.

This is not to deny that there are qualities of good in human nature. There are, we know full well, native impulses to tenderness, to courage, to sympathy and heroism. But they are strangely intermingled with capacities for evil, so that the task of the educator and the social reformer is to evoke the one and seek to overcome the other. Yet experience seems to show that there are limits set to the possibility of doing so. The creation of a new environment alone is not sufficient. The need for it is clamant enough, God knows—better homes, healthier surroundings, more parental responsibility, wiser teachers, discerning psychotherapy. But in the end the raw material of human nature may baffle the best intentions, and the new personality it was sought to evoke never emerge! In their massive volumes: *Soviet Communism, A New Civilization*, the Webbs have a chapter entitled: *The Re-making of Man*. One reads it with intense interest, but with a final scepticism. It describes a vast array of planned social services designed to offer a higher standard of life to the Russian people. Possibly in many ways this has been obtained, and aptitudes for life previously thwarted may have been evoked. One would not wish for a moment to decry such likelihood. Then comes the devastating question: And has the nature of the Russian people been changed? The answer to that is more dubious. Life under the new regime was designed to evoke new aptitudes for common service and a new sense of liberty. In practice the regime proves to be a grim regimentation where even inner freedom is suppressed and men live in constant fear and dread of suspicion, denunciation and purging. Reactions to that must inevitably be either dull submission and repression or slowly burning inner fires of rebellion.

The Christian view of human nature is at once more radical and more realistic. It has a high conception of what man was designed to be and the purpose of his existence: higher than any other of all the philosophies and religions. " Made in the image of God "—something godlike about him—in his perilous endowment of freedom, shall we say, his intelligence, his capacity for responsibility? Born, too, if the word of the New Testament be received, to become the child of God by grace as he is by creation, and the heir of eternal life. We recall again the stately and majestic words of the answer to the first question of the Shorter Catechism: " The chief end of man is to glorify God and enjoy Him for ever! " Did human imagination ever soar higher in its view of the dignity of man?

Yet on any view of the facts the mordant verdict must be written: Of that high destiny he has fallen far short. Men's misuse of their freedom, prostitution of their intelligence to base ends, repudiation of responsibility for their deeds or the outcome of them, are written deep on the records of history. Whatever likeness to God lies in man's nature it is scarred, broken and disfigured: shame and guilt are the only fitting emotions the sorry tale can call forth! Man is a sinner!

In this condition the common man shares like the rest of men. The frailties of human nature are his also. His sins are not worse than the sins of others, but they are sins! True, he has been often greatly sinned against: he has also sinned against his own kind and others. If the immoralities of kings appal us, so do those of which the common man is capable. If the profligacies of wealth and nobility repel us, is not the common man also the slave of his vices —intemperance, gambling, sex perversion, bestiality, brutality and the like? If avarice has stalked with greedy step amongst the employing class, can it not also be found as starkly in the heart of the common man?

This is our human situation to which religion speaks most profoundly, and the word is to the common man as to every other man! Here is the supreme demonstration that religion has its own independent roots in the need and nature of man. From this sinful condition which bows us with shame and guilt we need to be "redeemed", and only religion can do it. The peculiar glory of the Christian religion is that it addresses itself to this situation first of all. It brings our sin home to us, discovers to us the difference between what we are and what we ought to be, bows us with shame before a righteousness we have not attained and a goodness we do not possess, moves us to subduing wonder and awe—the very sense of the "numinous"—before the presence of a holy God within us who is pressing our sin and shame upon us and yet wooing us with His love to better things. This is the real re-making of man, a new man created by the transfer of his affection from self to God as the centre of his being: what Christians call "new life in Christ" and in this the soul of reverence is stirred to its fulness.

The one indispensable condition of our attaining it is the candid confession of our sinfulness. That is not easy for the common man or any other. We are prone to be easy with our own faults though moved to hardness with the sins of others. The modern man, it has been said, has a very easy conscience. "I've been unfaithful to my wife, but I make naught of that," said a rebellious son of labour, "but I do think there's something wrong with the economic system." We can only say that if he first felt the shame of his infidelity to his wife, he would have more right to challenge the economic wrongs of himself and his class. An aboriginal tribe on the borders of the province of Yunnan in S.W. China won to the Christian way of life from a state of oppression and moral degradation had more sense of the reality of the matter. They were sometimes

asked to describe the pre-Christian life from which they had
been delivered. They could never be brought to do it. It
was too indescribable for words: the very remembrance
made them shudder. So, too, from India comes the remark
of an old man belonging to the tribe of the Khonds of
Orissa: " Before the missionary came we were like the
beasts of the field; but now we believe in Jesus Christ."

Religion as we have described it, therefore, has three
outstanding words for the common man. The first word
confronts him with the fact of Christ, the supreme revelation of God and His purpose to the world. The second
faces him with the wonder of the universe and the mystery
of our existence therein, and sets Christ before him as the
explanation of the wonder and the clue to the mystery.
The third brings the common man face to face with the
mystery of his own sinful nature and its need, and points
to Christ again as the one sure minister to that need and the
one unfailing source of redemption and new life. These
three words to the common man are humbling in the
extreme, as they are to every man. Yet if he will but hearken
and believe, they are sure words of his uplifting.

VII

HOW RELIGION COMES TO THE COMMON MAN

WHATEVER THE SCEPTICS, critics and traducers of religion say, religion does come to the common man. The religious people in the world are mostly common people, drawn from the toilers and often enough from the poor and dispossessed. This in face of all contrary signs and all opposing forces; even despite the fact that some appear utterly irreligious and that masses of folk seem untouched by any religious influence or feeling.

I

With the common man as with others, religion appears in a great variety of guises and on many different levels. Much of it is pagan and primitive. Some is crude and rankly superstitious. A good deal of it is irrational, incited by intense and disturbing emotional appeals. But some of it is clear-sighted, shot through with a degree of intelligent apprehension and often informed with a desire to know more and understand better—a quality that is of itself often the product of the religious influence. At this level it provides the foundation of high moral character. It can issue in idealism, a strong sense of duty and public service.

Of the truth of this, history and experience offer ample testimony. From primitive folk upward, religion in one form or another is everywhere to be found influencing the life of peoples and nations. The great religions have their roots far back in antiquity, and in the course of their long history have affected the lives of literally millions upon millions of the human race generation after generation. The anti-God museums of Soviet Russia bear witness to the fact. Whether the effect of the sum total of religion in its various guises has been for good or ill is not so easy to say: it is not all white, nor all black, and a great deal of it is mottled grey. If, greatly daring, we venture a generalization, it would be that the sanctions of religion are a great social bond, and when these sanctions decline and are not replaced by religious sanctions of a higher order, the social bond tends to dissolve. Not only the morality, but the verve of a people, the will to live, will be undermined. If the heart of religion be, as we conceive it, a faith which faces the mystery and meaning of life with conviction born of a sense of supernatural aid, the decline of such faith can only mean a weakening of the social fabric that rests upon it and a demoralization of those who trusted it. From such straits the only remedy is the movement to a higher faith. The other alternative: that, if there be no supernatural aid, and faith in it be a delusion, we must rest on our unaided human wit and strength, is counsel of despair. Human life, then, becomes void of ultimate meaning or purpose, and we are but " the busy tribes of flesh and blood ", carried downward by the flood of time to be lost in following years!

What evidence have we that religion, possessing its own truth and value in varying degree, has had significance for the particular situation of the common man? The social systems of the great empires of antiquity, Assyria, Babylon, Persia, Egypt, Greece and Rome, were broad-based on the backs of vast slave populations. In the nature of the case, it is hard to say what religion did for them—the slaves of the slave market of Delos, or the Helots of Sparta, the forced labourers who built the Pyramids or the diverse slave elements in the make-up of ancient Rome. They have left no records to tell us, and in this case only such evidence would be adequate: ancient codes of law, like those of Hammurabi or of Rome, testify to some concern for the lot of the slave, but Epictetus seems the solitary slave who has left a memorial behind him.

Yet out of this dumb vast mass of accumulated human misery, there do come two pieces of enlightening testimony. Hebrew religion, the religion of the Old Testament, in which both Judaism and Christianity have their roots, has the peculiar distinction that it was the religion of a nation of liberated slaves. When Hebrew fathers answered their sons' questions about their origins, they were told to say: "We were Pharaoh's bondmen in Egypt; and the Lord brought us up out of Egypt with a mighty hand." The counsels of Hebrew law concerning the treatment of Hebrew slaves and particularly their emancipation in the seventh year, turned on the remembrance of this historic fact. "When thou lettest him go free from thee, thou shalt not let him go empty; thou shalt furnish him liberally out of thy flock, and out of thy threshing floor, and out of thy winepress; as the Lord thy God hath blessed thee, thou shalt give unto him. And thou shalt remember that thou wast a bond man in the land of Egypt and the Lord thy God redeemed thee."[1] That call to remembrance breaks on the ear like a refrain through the whole of the Old Testament: it was the very nerve of the religion of the Hebrew people that they were a people redeemed by an act of the exceeding grace of God.

The other testimony comes from the ghettoes and slave quarters of ancient Graeco-Roman cities, like Rome, Corinth or Ephesus. When Christian faith made its appeal to the ancient world outside Palestine, it was among these levels of the population that it won its first adherents. Here a religion of redemption was making its own virgin appeal and finding response in those to whom it made it. The redemption was more than a gift of economic emancipation or political liberty, and it was long before those

1 Deut. 6.20-23.

issues ultimately inherent in its gospel were achieved. The message brought new life and hope to folk that were oppressed and dispossessed. By it their little lives were invested with a divine significance which reacted on the whole social fabric in which they lived, lifting them above its moral squalor and infusing into their relations with their neighbours a new grace, patience and purity. " Such were some of you," wrote St. Paul to his Corinthian converts, when detailing gross sins of the heathen world from which they had been delivered "washed clean," he says, "by the Spirit of our God."[2] He seems in the same letter almost to boast in their lowly worldly condition: " Behold your calling, brethren, how that not many wise after the flesh, not many mighty, not many noble: but God chose . . . foolish . . . weak . . . and base things, and things that are despised."[3]

Subsequent Christian history, in the Middle Ages and in modern times, has demonstrated the same power of appeal to the oppressed and dispossessed. Medieval popular movements like the Albigenses, the Waldensians, English peasantry in the time of Wat Tyler and Jack Ball, all tell of it. So does the story of the Christian religion among the slave populations of the West Indies and the Southern States of the U.S.A., and not less among the tribes of Africa and the outcastes of India. There is truth in the quip, half serious, half jesting: Christianity is the religion of all poor devils!

II

The jungle of undergrowth which the history of religion reveals is plentifully illustrated in the modern world: not least in the variety of forms the Christian religion has taken. In a single small Yorkshire town of some 15,000 souls, there could be enumerated not long ago nine Methodist chapels of four different varieties, three Anglican churches, two Baptist, one each to the Roman Catholics,

[2] I Cor. 6.11.　　　　　　[3] I Cor. 1.26-29.

Moravians, Congregationalists and Unitarians, together with small communities of the Christian Scientists and Seventh Day Adventists and in addition an occasional visitation by Mormon missionaries. Apart from a sprinkling of manufacturers and professional men, the bulk of the adherents of these religious groups were unmistakably working class.

If we look for further samples of religious diversity among ordinary men and women, then America is the land to which to turn. In his book, *Religion in America* (1945), Willard L. Sperry, Dean of the Divinity School at Harvard, quotes from the Federal Census of 1936, the figure of 256 religious denominations in the continent of the U.S.A. " The religious history of the United States is that of an ecclesiastical fecundity and fertility," he writes, " carried to a point which must distress any theologically minded Malthus. . . . This is a land, perhaps the only land in Christendom, which can spawn an Aimée McPherson and a Father Divine with wanton disregard of all the sober Christian conventions." He recalls that William James' famous work, *The Varieties of Religious Experience*, first appeared contemporaneously with a book by a popular American naturalist entitled *Wild Animals I have known*, and someone suggested that the proper title for James' book was " Wild Religions I have known ".

American diversity in religion is not difficult to explain. The American settlers, trying to leave Europe behind, in fact have taken its racial and religious divisions with them. Within little more than a century from the first settlements, Britain had exported Episcopacy and Puritanism, Independency and Quakerism, and Presbyterians and Catholics had found a new home, while from the Continent had come Huguenots, Dutch Reformers and German Lutherans. A little later were to come the Baptists and the Methodists, and after the War of Independence these were the sects who best kept pace with the movement of the frontier westwards over the Alleghanies and across the plains.

The fact of people liberated from old conventions for a new, adventurous and uncertain life goes far to explain the ranker growths of American religious sectarianism, where new forms of religion sprout with amazing rapidity. Hence the camp meetings of the frontier days, the plaintive exuberance of negro religion, a curious symbolism like that of a group of Kentucky farmers who practise snake-charming in their religious assemblies, the irrational Biblicism of Tennessee and the strange apparition of Brigham Young and the Mormon Church. Yet, written over the whole story, in its teeming and almost extravagant variety, is the fact that this is the religion of common men.

Yet another great land gives evidence of the religion of common men, to wit, Russia past and present. Paul Miliukov, in the first volume of his *Outlines of Russian Culture*, devotes three chapters to the schism which split the Orthodox Church in Russia into Orthodox and Old Believers, and these latter again into " Priestists " and "Priestless ". He follows these with a vivid chapter on *The Development of Russian Sectarianism*. The dispute which occasioned the schism was over missals and rituals, and whether those which had become customary and traditional in the Russian Church should be revised to bring them into line with developments in Greek counter-parts from which they had sprung. Should they, as did now the Greeks, hold two fingers in making the sign of the cross, or walk against the sun in ecclesiastical processions?

The separation, however, raised for the Old Believers a question as to how their religious needs could be met if deprived of the ministrations of orthodox clergy. Would not a new order of priests be necessary, or could they do without priests altogether? So arose the separatist church of the Old Believers, the "Priestists ", among whom Miliukov declares religion was freer and more spiritual. In the detachment of the latter from a ritual religion is to be found the ground on which the fertile growths of Russian sectarianism, stimulated by influences from Protestantism, sprang up. Religion was set free from ritual and credal tests, and could become both individual and mystical, irrational and ecstatic, evangelical and spiritual or inward. So arose the sects, the " Khlysty ", the " Skoptsy ", the " Molokans " (who drink only milk on fast days), the Sturdo-Baptists and the "Dukhobors" ("wrestlers of the Spirit "), whose diversity makes such a fascinating contri-bution to the study of religion. Among the Stundists and Dukhobors particularly the attempt was made to repudiate the existing social order, and establish a religio-com-munistic society, holding property in common, and refusing obedience to government in the matter of taxes and military service. The popular character of these developments is the point at issue: both in the Orthodox Church and in the sects here were forms of religion to which the " common man " gravitated.

To find a road for the understanding through this jungle of religious diversity, our best guide is possibly that religious thinker of insight, Baron von Hügel. He distinguishes three elements in religion, the cult, the faith and theology which seek to make it intelligible, and the inward personal apprehension of the truth of religion with its outgoings in " experimental-ethical life ". Variation in religion may enter with each element. The cult may change: the Sacra-ment of the Mass may give place to the Preaching of the Word and that again to silent waiting on God in Quaker meeting. Diversity of emphasis may come in the faith and the reasoned theology of it, and Justification by Faith take the place of priestly absolution. Or new faith may supplant the old, as when Christianity arose in the place of Judaism. There is room for variation in personal apprehension and experience of the truth of religion: Catholic devotion and Protestant piety, the glow of vivid evangelical experience or the Quaker's calm serenity in possession of the " inner light ". Some concession also may be made to the grain of truth in the Marxian view of religion, that temporal circum-stance—not economic alone—may at least affect, colour and condition the quality and character of religious experience, and differentiate the religion of primitive man from that of civilized man, and that of a college don from that of a Christian miner at the coal face. But God has many children, and varied ways of making Himself known to them, according to their capacity and aptitude.

III

There are many ways in which the truth and power of religion take hold of common men, and are vindicated in their experience. Varied as the guises and expressions of religion are, there is a generic quality about all religious experience: a common fact expressed in a variety of ways, namely, the arrest by and awakening to the reality and presence of God. The experience kindles awe, reverence, humility, wonder, adoration, rapture, praise and joy—according to the content of the revelation and the human need to which it is the response. Here the revealing word lights up the baffling mystery of human existence; there it brings deliverance from inward sin and frustration; in yet another case it summons the slumbering soul to adventurous service for God and man. The awareness may come catastrophically or gradually, but in every case there is some sense of being arrested, brought up against a presence not our own, more than human in fact, with which we must come to terms, for, in the language of the 139th Psalm, it "besets us behind and before".

Within the circles of Protestant Christianity—to speak here of no other—there are three classic cases of religion thus coming to men of the common people: Luther, Fox and Bunyan. Of these there is no need to speak at length, for their stories are well known, and their testimonies have been scrutinized to the last letter in the psychologies of religious experience. This judgment only must be registered, that the experience of these men clearly illustrates that religion has its own independent roots. It is not an offshoot of economic condition or temporal circumstance however much it may be affected by these in its outworking. Luther's turning to religion and his entry into the monastery were occasioned by the sudden death of a friend, which raised for him the question of the meaning of life here and hereafter. In the case of Fox we detect an unrest evoked by the evil and violence of the times which drove him, clad in leathern jerkin, to wander over Midland England seeking light with which to subdue the evil: not finding repose until he saw " the infinite ocean of light above the ocean of darkness ". Bunyan, by his own confession, was a poor man and remained so, but, if what he writes in *Grace Abounding to the Chief of Sinners* is true, it was not his poverty which drove him to make his peace with God, but his desperate sense of sin. In each of these classic cases, if the phrase be allowed, it was an inner sense of *malaise,* desperate " unease " about the mystery of life, the power of evil and the sense of sin which evoked recourse to God, and called for trust in Him as the one way of release and health. The Christian faith was showing itself to be a religion of inward redemption !

The greatest religious awakening of modern times was the eighteenth-century Evangelical Revival in England, the fruit of which may be seen in all the earth and is not yet exhausted. Social historians freely admit the fact, and are not slow to point out that its great appeal was to the industrial classes of England: the fishermen and tin miners of Cornwall, the miners of Kingswood, Northumberland and Durham, the steel and iron workers of Birmingham and Sheffield and textile workers of East Lancashire and the West Riding. The character of the religious appeal, however, is often caricatured and, indeed, misrepresented. It was not primarily an appeal to fear, but to surrender to a loving and holy God. Wesley's supreme theme was " holiness ", his aim " to spread scriptural holiness through the land ", and " holiness " means " wholeness ", the wholeness and wholesomeness of life in the love of God. That sometimes the terrors of hell were vividly portrayed is doubtless true, but that was to make men feel " the exceeding sinfulness of sin " and to make them desire to be delivered from it. The aim of all the preaching was to turn men from sin to righteousness, from self to love of God and man. Heaven, whether here or hereafter, was not the reward of virtue, but the blessedness of new life in Christ, born of simple trust. To describe religion of such a kind as a product of economic forces is simply preposterous!

Our concern, however, is with the way religion comes to common men to-day. For come it does, sometimes in the most casual way. A remarkable case was discovered in a mining village in north-west England, and the man himself is as remarkable as his story. A week-end in his home revealed a mind of remarkable power, knowledge and insight. He knew the history of the British working-class movement from A to Z, and something of the continental story also. He had the Marxian philosophy at his fingertips. And he was " steward " at the local Methodist chapel. " How did religion come to you? " he was asked. " Someone asked me to sing in the chapel for a special service," was the reply. For years he had been living a wild, reprobate and revolutionary life, his chief evening relaxation singing and drinking in local public-houses. Something in the contrast between chapel life and the life he had been living struck him, and religion took possession of him. He could say no more than that, but his religion glows in every word he speaks.

From the west Midlands comes another record of an almost casual episode which turned a man to religion. The man is a Christian man, known for the sterling integrity of his character, his zeal for social righteousness and the influence he exerts on a wide circle of his contemporaries. At the core of his religion is a passionate devotion to the Person of Christ, or, as he himself puts it, to " Jesus ". Born in a working-class home, which was warmly attached to the local chapel, the turning point in his career came at about seventeen years of age. If you ask him about it, he will tell you of an occasion when he was seeing a minister of religion off at the local railway station. The minister in question must have read the unrest in the lad's heart. Ere he departed, he went to the bookstall and purchased a daily paper. He handed this to the lad, saying as he did so: "Here H——, see what a mess men are making of my Father's world!"

Two testimonies to the character of working-class religion and the inner *malaise* that drives men to it have come in recent years from Mr. J. J. Lawson, now Lord Lawson. One is his own twice-printed autobiography, *A Man's Life*, in the reading of which the late Lord Tweedsmuir confessed such delight. The other is his vivid biography of Peter Lee, Methodist local preacher and miners' leader, a name to be conjured with in County Durham, so much so that a whole new town is to be named after him. A curious likeness appears in the turning to religion of these two men of Durham mining villages. Of himself at the turning from irreligion to religion, Lord Lawson writes: "Silently, subtly, almost unconsciously I had been building a barrier between myself and my old gambling habits and rough and ready life—an intellectual and moral barrier." After describing how he withdrew himself from his old haunts, and, taking to books in his yearning for education, was "voted queer" by those around him, he continues: "Apart from the meagre elementary education, one great force held the field in the matter of personal development—and that was the chapel. And looking back now, I see that it was inevitable that I should ultimately seek the company of the serious-minded people who gravitated together and formed the 'Society'."

A similar *malaise* with an old bad life also moved Peter Lee. There can be few more vivid life-stories than that of Peter Lee's first thirty-three years, when he was known for his drinking and fighting, had suffered as an "agitator", and sought escape from economic poverty in America and

Africa. What inner unrest was it that turned him from his manner of life until then to a quite different one? Lord Lawson attributes the change to the influence of his mother. " There had come to him something deeper than experience won in the world of men, that which was so upheaving that it definitely marks a change in him and his outlook. That quiet, wise character—dominating, indwelling mother of his had come out at last. . . . If strangers who met that mother remember the elevating power of her presence, how could one born of her stay free of it? " So he turned to religion. " Religion," says Lord Lawson, " made a profound change in Peter Lee. Not churches, creeds or sermons, but that inner experience which recks not of such things. And just as surely as men have turned their backs upon the world for some retreat, so did this man give himself, body and soul, to the new way of life. Men wondered to see him: and none wondered more than himself."

Testimonies multiply till they are too many for lengthy description. Here it is a tale of change that happened catastrophically after a long period of " unconscious cerebration ", as the psychologists call it, like the stories of " Old Drunk " and the London Tube motor-driver of whom Harold Begbie told years back in *Broken Earthenware*. There, from a Yorkshire industrial village, comes a man's story of the influence of his father that shaped in the man himself a love of God and the things which belong to God. Still again from the Cheviots comes the tale of a man's hand laid in blessing on a boy's head, leaving a mark on the boy's spirit that, nearly sixty years after, he can still recall. For others, it is the contagion of a great emotion sweeping through a whole community as the fires of revival break out into holy flame.

What is the content of faith which sustains such religion? In its evangelical setting, it is most often a vivid apprehension of inner necessity to " get right with God ", and a sure sense that God has come near to men in Jesus Christ, liberated them from inner unrest about what they are, and

F

given them power to live a new life. Its highest pitch is echoed in a hymn of the eighteenth-century revival which still survives.

> And can it be that I should gain
> An interest in the Saviour's blood?
> Died He for me, who caused Him pain?
> For me, who Him to death pursued?
> Amazing love! How can it be
> That Thou, my God, shouldst die for me?

A later verse in the hymn describes the sense of liberation experienced.

> Long my imprisoned spirit lay
> Fast bound in sin and nature's night.
> Thine eye diffused a quickening ray,
> I woke, the dungeon flamed with light.
> My chains fell off, my heart was free.
> I rose, went forth, and followed Thee!

An occasion is reported when a company of Durham miners, who knew by experience the joy of their inner liberation, sang those last two lines over, not once, or twice, or thrice, but twenty-two times! But would the experience which evoked such rapture have been essentially different with the East End workers whom Father Groser gathers to the Communion Table hard by St. Katherine's docks: or with the Parisian *gamins* whom Abbé Godin won for the love of Jesus in *Pagan France*?

What are the issues of such religion in the lives of common men? Lord Lawson says that the eighteenth-century Revival " saturated the industrial masses with a passion for a better life, personal, moral, mental and social ". A week-end in a Derbyshire working-man's home amply illustrates what this means. Just a Council house, with father—a pattern-maker in a neighbouring iron works—mother and two eager-spirited boys to make up the family. In that home there is culture: a small library of good books that would have done credit to many a well-to-do home. In the family circle, there was peace, affection, sobriety, cleanliness, and a sense of the presence of God. From that home emanated friendship and a spirit of service. The man was a trusted member of his trade union: and both husband and wife were leaders in the work of a village chapel and its Sunday-school. The week-end in that home was a pure delight. There religion was doing its perfect work.

VIII

THE COMMON MAN AND HIS WORK

FROM EARLIEST AGES up to civilized times, the rudimentary problem of the common man has been how he should be fed, housed and clothed. Because he is a creature of nature with a physical body to keep alive, he must gather his food from the fruits of the earth, from land, cattle and the denizens of the sea, build a shelter of sticks, leaves or mud, and clothe himself from plant fibres or the skins, fur or wool of beasts. Only dwellers in isles of the Southern Seas have ever been reputed to be able to exist without laborious toil, and even there the legend is largely fictitious. In highly developed and organized communities, the basic problem is still the same: more complex in its working out, but at bottom identical with that of the caveman. The modern city dweller's brick house, with all the newest gadgets, is answer to the same necessity as brings into being the mud huts, thatched with leaves, of an African kraal.

Around this basic question, much of the fret, unrest, and sense of injured justice that mark the labour of the world turn. Who shall do what? How shall the resultant product be divided up? On what principles? To what end? For what purpose? Some elusive and unsatisfactory answers have been given to those questions, at which we must look, for they account for the dissatisfaction which exists in the world of labour. In particular, religion, it is said, has little or nothing to say to the work of the world, or the way it is done. We must now face that challenge.

I

The relevance of religion to the work of the world, it has been shrewdly observed, is seen every Monday morning when the Christian man, refreshed by Sunday rest and worship, enters workshop, office, mine or factory, where, with other men, he takes his place in the workaday world to win his daily bread.

On many counts, it is a complex and testing world into which he enters. Modern industry is a vast and over-towering apparition compared with the simple economies of more primitive civilizations. The British Ministry of Labour schedules one hundred different trades and occupations in which the working population of Britain, numbering 23,000,000 souls, may engage, from farming to engineering and the distributive trades. Beyond these lie the professional callings of doctor, nurse, teacher and lawyer, and those engaged in national or local government.

The operations of modern industry are far-flung. Raw materials must be brought from the ends of the earth, to be manufactured into goods for the supply of human need, and then distributed to the markets where they are required. Industry and commerce thus present an intricate network of interdependent relations between the peoples of the earth, as a reflective glance at the way a modern breakfast table is furnished and replenished will amply demonstrate.

No less fascinating is the technical aspect of modern industry. This is, we are repeatedly told, an age of technics. When the modern worker steps into his work-shop or factory, he is greeted by a world of machines: automatic looms, machine tools, lathes, presses, boring machines, hammers, levers, cranes, endless belts and hoists. The age of the craftsman passes, the age of the machine-minder dawns. If we are determined by the tools we use, as the Marxians say, we are likely to become a race of mechanical men. Even the bank clerk turns to the type-writer and the comptometer. The transformation to the machine age has come so swiftly, that we have hardly had time to grasp its full significance for good or ill. This much we can say. Much donkey-work has been transferred from human shoulders to the machine, production has multiplied in some cases a thousand-fold, and human needs can more easily be met. But introduction of machines has often displaced labour and created a new problem of unemployment, nor has the machine eliminated all dirty, disagreeable or laborious toil, and it is on occasion itself a producer of noise and dirt. Yet no one will doubt that machines bear eloquent testimony to our increasing facility to use natural power and resource to greater human advantage. But they may be, and in some sense are, even in their highest creations such as the *Queen Elizabeth* and the *Brabazon*, nothing more than clever mechanical gadgets and devices which serve our greater convenience and help more easily to supply our temporal needs. While they bring us increased control over natural resources, they do nothing to solve the mystery of human existence. They may, indeed, add to it, as when the discovery of atomic energy opens up an appalling vista of evil it may do if wrongly used. That, however, is not a question of technics, but of moral control, which leads us to another aspect of the matter.

II

Modern industry is not only a world of machines: it is also a world of men and women toiling side by side for daily bread. The human side of the problem of industry is more testing than the technical. Machines may solve the problem of production, and, granted that the fertility of the earth proves sufficient for the increasing size of the human race, eliminate scarcity and want. They will not solve the problem of human relations in industry or anywhere else. For the men and women engaged in industry are sinful folk like the rest of us. This is the cause of the sores of the industrial world, whose history is the story of perverse and sinful relations between the various partners in industry, and the wrongs they have mutually enacted on one another. Here some of the raw deficiencies of human nature reveal themselves in their ugliest guise. Sloth, avarice, dishonesty, envy, injustice, disregard of one's fellows, contempt and exploitation of the weak, inhumanity and barbarity almost beyond compare, have made the story of human industry a very black record down to our own time. The picture is scarcely relieved by occasions when the milk of human kindness has stirred, or when the sense of affronted justice has awakened on behalf of the oppressed and wronged.

The ground of the human tension in industry lies in the elementary condition of our existence. Human life is precarious and uncertain, and far from ever being socially " secure ". Part of the insecurity rests in the necessity to labour for daily bread. The seemingly harsh word of St. Paul is, after all, a rescript of our elementary condition. " If a man will not work, neither shall he eat." In the sweat of their brow, must men labour for the physical means of their existence.

The situation is not entirely relieved by the recognition that labour is always in some degree a communal enterprise. Primitive people work out their economy in families, clans and tribal groups—hunt, fish and herd cattle together, and in agricultural communities allot the land and determine what shall be the individual's contribution to and share in the common larder. From the commencement there is division of labour, different callings to different men—and occasion of strife between different callings on that account. In time these divergences harden into class or caste distinctions. When the elemental needs of human existence are met, the economy may permit of the slow emergence of a leisured, but not necessarily idle, class, which can develop the interests of religion, culture and learning. So, in a complex civilization like that of ancient Babylon, a priestly class emerged, who could study the stars in their courses and map out the constellations for the guidance of mankind. But in the emergence of such divergent interests between different groups in the community lay the ground of struggle and dispute.

The precarious and uncertain character of man's existence evokes some of the worst traits of human nature. The instinct of self-preservation will make us tend to ignore or neglect our brother's need. Because labour is arduous and toilsome, there is the temptation for the slothful to dodge their fair share of it, and for the strong to thrust the burden of it upon the weak. Thus emerged the shameful wrong of slavery which has persisted down to our own time. The vanquished in war might be spared their life that they might till their conqueror's fields, like the Helots of Sparta and the captive slaves of Imperial Rome. Or avarice might prompt the greedy creditor to claim the enslavement of the debtor, to work off the impossible debt. Did not the farmers of Judah in Micah's day exclaim that they were flayed to the bone and their flesh chopped off for the stew-pot? Yet the infliction of slavery appears not to have relieved the burden of human toil, but to have intensified it, even for those who inflicted it. The Spartans had to be perpetually on guard lest the Helots rebel against them; and Rome went in continual fear of slave uprisings; as South Africans and Americans to-day are in constant dread of what would happen if the black races they have oppressed should ever appeal to force to right their wrongs. So grim a Nemesis comes upon injustice done in the work of the world.

The modern industrial worker, in principle, is no slave, but a free man, able to sell his labour where he will. The neatest definition of the free economy known as Capitalism is that of Weber: the organization of free labour by the inducement of wages for the sake of profit. This made the tie between worker and employer a "cash nexus", so much pay for so much work, and wages, the price of labour, became a matter of constant haggling and argument. In the initial stages, the individual worker, in days when

labour was abundant, found himself beaten down in the
price of his labour, and faced with the dilemma between
low, inadequate wages and long hours or unemployment.
In conflict about wages and hours, the worker was driven
to combine with his fellows, and to that extent human
brotherhood found some expression. Combination among
the workers, however, led to the inevitable reaction, combination among employers, and industry became organized, as
it were, in two opposing camps: and the battle of wages and
hours pursued its embittered course. In that conflict, the
ends which human industry should serve often disappeared
from view, and the interests of community and consumer
were neglected or forgotten.

From this impasse, escape only seemed to offer along
two roads. One was to protect the workers, the weaker
side in the conflict, by factory acts which regulated hours,
wages and other conditions, and by insurance provisions
against sickness, unemployment and old age, and assistance
in care of the family. These ultimately issued in the conception of the " welfare state " and a policy of full employment—more jobs than men—which removes the fear of
unemployment. The other road was indicated by the increasing demand of Socialist and Marxian theories alike
that the State should take over and manage land and industry in behalf of the whole community. Industry was
thus to be a communal enterprise, and men were to find
the incentive to labour in service of the community.

Candour compels the judgment that the day of salvation
for industry is not assured along either line, however inevitable either development may appear to be. The latent
evil in human nature asserts itself along both, frustrating
the achievement of the desired end. Conflict about wages
and hours goes on in the " welfare state ". Social services
are abused, the policy of full employment leads the worker
naturally to prefer the clean job to the dirty job, and labour
shortage means idle machines and reduced production.
Instead of a higher standard of life, we are threatened with

a lower one. The one redeeming feature is that if the latter result ensues, we may have to learn to be poor together.

Nor is it clear that communal enterprise, whether in "Communist" Russia, or "Socialized" Britain, can evoke strongly or effectively the incentive of service to the community. It is there—but vaguely, nebulously and irresolutely. In the one case, there are specious efforts to arouse keenness in labour, like "Stakhanovism", or an appeal to the sentiment of national patriotism, or the attempt to compel it by the imposition of forced labour euphemistically described as "socially educative". In the other case, we witness an epidemic of arbitrary and unofficial strikes— careless of ill done to the community—and sinister symptoms of a struggle for power by unscrupulous forces. Before such facts, it is sheer folly to talk of " the essential goodness of human nature ", or to think that by changing conditions, however justly, we necessarily change men. Human nature remains what it was, a strange mixture of good and ill, and other forces are needed to evoke the good and restrain the ill.

This, however, is the world of actualities in which the modern industrial worker does his daily work. He has not only materials to handle and machines to manage. He must also adjust himself to his fellow-workers. Nor is it a simple matter of treating them as fellow-men and women, and finding expression for human regard and good fellowship. He meets them in a variety of relations: as managers, foremen, shop-stewards, fellow trade unionists, employers or customers. Simple human relationships, the man-to-man attitude, may be obscured by the very complexity of functions and capacities in which he has to do with them. There are all sorts of snags to be encountered. In industry, people are brought together in a co-operative effort to supply certain human needs. It is therefore first a question of efficiency at various levels: capable management, good workmanship and so on. If these are lacking there will be fret and irritation. There are divergences of outlook on life: class suspicions and hostilities, political differences, differences in moral attitudes to right and wrong, and religious differences—religion and irreligion—all of which make simple human fellowship acutely difficult. Only when some situation arises—an accident in a factory, a colliery explosion, or, wider still, a common national peril like a state of war—are people in industry lifted above the interests which divide them and the elemental humanities break through.

With all our technical advances and social planning, therefore, modern industry still presents us with a problem as yet unresolved, of imperfect relations between imperfect and sinful men. A worker once described industry as he knew it as "a jungle", so dense was the undergrowth of conflicting interests. An employer roundly declared: "industry is war", so acute was the dispute about just distribution. The Marxists have some justification for speaking of a "class struggle". While it is not the whole story, history bears witness to its existence and reality.

Worst of all, there is a conspicuous lack of a pervasive sense of the purpose which industry should serve, that runs up into the absence of a faith that gives meaning and purpose to life. Reliable testimony from a Midland city tells of a board of directors in conference with chief officials and foremen, posing the question: "What is work for?" and failing to find a satisfactory answer. The case is possibly extreme, but significant. Ask anyone in the world of industry, high or low, why they go to work, and the cases where you get any answer beyond a self-regarding one will be few or far between.

There is no ultimate meaning in work done for purely self-regarding motives. Any apparent meaning disappears before the ruthless question: "Why should your life be worth preserving?" On the naturalistic scheme of things there is no reason for self-preservation, and no ultimate goal for our work if this life be all. On this basis we are nothing more than a more or less thriving race of earth-worms. Nor does a merely this-worldly philosophy like that of the Marxians serve any better. Why live for a community life yet to be realized generations ahead, which may never come to pass, and even if it does, in the tran-science of human affairs, will most certainly pass away again? In this desperate impasse, we turn to enquire whether religion can help us.

III

What then is the relevance of religion to this situation? Some quite clear and definite affirmations may be made.

(i) Religion supplies, as nothing else, a sense of divine purpose for the work of the world. Our work can only have meaning so far as it serves the purpose for which human life exists. Man, on the religious view, is born for communion with God, and his ultimate destiny is eternal. Toil is necessary to man's temporal life—he must work if he would eat, and he must eat if he would continue to live on earth—but it gets out of its perspective if it does not serve the eternal end of his being. Hence, to the religious man, work is an offering to the eternal glory of God.

There is, in fact, something sacramental about it. The raw materials which we handle—be they the fruits of soil, sea or mine, or the precious material of human souls which a teacher or a minister of religion handles—are of God's creation, and therefore sacred. In work we handle holy things as truly as any priest at the altar, emblems of a divine life imparted to us and consecrated by our toil. Religious men feel that their work is " sacred ", because they are blending their labour with God's. So an East Riding farmer was heard to say: " Man, it's grand to be working on God's earth."

Some callings, it will be said, make it easy to believe and feel this, but conditions in others are against it. The difficulty may be granted, but is not insuperable. Coal-mining, for example, is especially arduous, and conditions underground often testing beyond words. " Can God really mean a man to work in such conditions? " said a miner, as sweat poured from him and the mire of the mine clung to him. But if work involved no mental or physical hardship, peril or discomfort, hardly any worth-while work would be done. A doctor must face nauseating symptoms of foul disease, social workers endure incredible discomfort when battling with the evils of the slums, and sailors and fishermen perpetually take their lives in their hands. Nor do all miners feel or speak as the one just mentioned. Many can be found who take pride in the value of their work to the community, some learn to joy in the story of coal that harnesses the energy of the sun which they in turn release, and one at least was heard to exclaim: " It's great to be a Christian at the coal face."

(ii) Work, to the religious man, is not only a gesture towards God; it is also an outgoing towards his fellows. It serves a dual purpose: the service of man alongside the glory of God. One test of the validity of our labour is that it really serves some human need. Very few callings cannot survive that test. It is dubious whether that of the book-maker can, who lives by exploiting the follies of his fellows. It is certain that of the procurer cannot, who prostitutes human lives to please the lusts of men. Beyond these, from the work of the farmer to that of the statesman, human labour is shot through with meaning when there is need to be met and service to be rendered, in which the work in question finds its justification.

Service to human need delivers work from the self-regarding interest which so often is the only or chief motive which sustains it. There is something disquieting about the common attitude to daily work. Very few can give a reason for it beyond that of necessity to earn their living or to provide for home and family. The first is obvious, but purely self-regarding, and seldom envisages the idea that we earn our own living most justifiably by helping other

people to live. The second motive—of maintaining a family
—has a worthier ring, but fails to recognize any obligation
beyond one's own family. Yet it needs only a little imagination to realize that since it takes the labour of the rest of
the world to supply our needs—as the very clothes on our
backs show—our justification for receiving that service is
that we contribute in return to supply the needs of our
fellows.

Work thus becomes a fulfilment of the second great
commandment, as it is of the first: Thou shalt love thy
neighbour as thyself. This helps also to deliver our work
from the meaninglessness which so often appears to envelop
it. Work is without adequate meaning if it serve no end
beyond ourselves. But if it be truly service of the temporal
or spiritual needs of our fellow man, service to his body,
his mind or his spirit, it begins to glow with meaning and
purpose. And if we remember that our neighbour, known
or unknown, whom we serve by our labour, is one born to
be a child of the living God, our work receives a touch of
eternal meaning. Work can so be raised to be a real
symbol of the brotherhood of mankind in God, and becomes
a token of the love we bear to that brotherhood. So seen,
the humblest of callings may be redeemed and exalted. A
Lancashire lad, working at a conveyor belt—often regarded
as the nadir of meaningless labour—caught a glimpse of
such meaning in his work in a Sunday afternoon talk. The
next day at noon, he said to his foreman: " Harold, I don't
know how it is, but my work seems altogether different
this morning."

(iii) When work is thus fortified by a sense of divine
purpose, other problems fall into their proper perspective,
and their solution is easier. There is, for example, a
religious man's choice of a calling, so far as that is possible
in the circumstances and opportunities of the contemporary
situation. Since he believes that his work, as well as his
life, is of interest to God, he will look for divine guidance.
He will find a real measure of it in the opportunities which

present themselves—we may remember the hundred different trades scheduled by the British Ministry of Labour—and by consideration of what he is most fitted for, by temperament, disposition, native talent or aptitude. The supreme consideration will be where is the need greatest, that is, where he with his gifts and aptitudes, however humble, can best serve. Need, call and opportunity may take him to the very ends of the earth, and mobility, as well as stability, of labour both lie in the purpose of God.

The same sense of purpose to be served will prompt not only his choice of avocation but also the spirit in which the religious man goes to his work day by day. There is a well-known hymn, sometimes known as the hymn of the Christian carpenter, which begins:

> Forth in Thy name, O Lord, I go
> My daily labour to pursue,
> Thee, only Thee, resolved to know,
> In all I think or speak or do!

Christian working men in Britain have been known to set out for their daily work humming those words to sustain and fortify their hearts for what lay in front of them. The results of such an attitude have been in integrity of character, faithfulness in work, trustworthiness in discharge of responsibility, keenness of judgment in facing issues that arise, and willingness to render disinterested service. Often enough it has won the confidence of fellow-workmen and employers not so minded. London dock-workers, by no means religiously minded, have been known to choose unanimously the one man among them known for his upright Christian character to fill a position of trust in their common service.

(iv) The possession of religious faith is no necessary guarantee of technical skill, but it may inspire a genuine desire to acquire it, that better service may thereby be rendered. Self-interest often inspires a like desire, but the different motive qualifies the worthiness of the aspiration.

The Christian working man has a deeper incentive to become a workman that needeth not to be ashamed, because his work is part of his religion, the materials he uses are of God's creation, and his native skill is God's gift to him. The combination of religious faith and technical ability makes for a rare order of craftsmanship. In a slate quarry in north Cornwall, the most skilled occupation was that of making lighthouse floors—perfectly round, perfectly smooth—to bear the lighthouse lamp. Not a generation ago, the man who was entrusted with that responsible work was known not only as a skilled craftsman but also as a devoutly religious man. You had only to see him at his work to know that sainthood and craftsmanship were there in a rare combination.

(v) Finally, what of the bearing of religion on the vexed question of the control and direction of industry? This is the point at which human sin has most disfigured the work of the world—by the conflicts of avarice, the exploitation of life and labour, by dishonesty, sloth and self-seeking. The religious man at least has to beware of falling prey to such sins himself, and to be ready to take part in the struggle against them as they operate in the industrial field. Because the fruits of the earth are to be garnered for the use of all God's children, he will be urgent to secure a just distribution thereof, and to ensure that none of God's children go hungry or ill-bestead. Because man is made in the image of God, he will be on guard against injustice or wrong, and the exploitation of life and labour which degrades man's native dignity. Social justice and human liberty will be the dual objects of his concern: as when George Loveless, leader of the Tolpuddle Martyrs, who suffered so wrongfully for combining to raise the wages of agricultural labourers from eight to ten shillings a week—the concern of social injustice—also wrote from prison:

We will, we will be free!

What should be the judgment of a religious man on the

issue as between a free economy and state control and direction of industry? The considerations are so manifold, that a clear and direct answer is not easy. The supreme question is: under which system will he be best able to work for the glory of God and the service of men? Obviously he ought to be able so to work under either system. The decision as to which best enables him to do so is matter of experience as to which system most advances social justice and human liberty. The problems will be different under each. Evils eliminated by the one are likely to appear in the other. Under free economy, the besetting sins are avarice and denial of human solidarity—each man for himself! Under the alternative system, denial of essential liberty and forced labour raise their sinister heads in the effort to compel a brotherhood between men—each for all, and all for each—which can only grow from within. Hence the religious man can be under no delusion that either a system of free economy or of state control and direction of industry will rid the work of the world of sin. The sins will be different, but they will be there, and no law of man can eradicate them: only the redeeming grace of God in the hearts of men can do that. For the religious man the task of directing his work to the glory of God and the service of man remains.

IX

RELIGION AND POLITICS

IF THE COMMON MAN's basic problem is how he shall be fed, housed and clothed, a closely related problem is how he shall be governed, or, shall we say, govern himself. In the modern world, economic problems turn to political questions. Governments more and more become vast community trading corporations and distributing agents. This is not to say that their other functions of maintaining law and order and administering justice are superseded: these functions are in fact both modified and extended by increasing power and responsibility in the economic field—with consequences still to be looked at.

Again the question of religion enters, this time in its bearing on politics. Here a curious divergence must be noted from the attitude to the bearing of religion on economics. To work, religion, it is said, is irrelevant: economics is merely a matter of how we deal with material things, get and spend, individually or collectively: and scientific management can be trusted to see to that. We have dealt with that fallacy, which so completely ignores the human factor and the sinfulness of man. But to politics and government, it is said, religion is a dangerous rival power, which must be curbed and subordinated, if not altogether suppressed. So much we may judge from the attitude of modern totalitarian states, be they communist, fascist or national-socialist.

This again is an issue which concerns the common man: if only because he has achieved political power, and is inclined to put a pathetic trust in the exercise of that power as the instrument of his redemption. By political action, gradual or revolutionary—he is encouraged to believe—all his wrongs will be righted and the perfect community be achieved. With that action religion must not be allowed to interfere. Into this judgment we must now look.

I

Government has always been a problem of extraordinary difficulty and complexity, which has nowhere been satisfactorily resolved, and perhaps fundamentally never can be. Its task is paradoxical, to compel by coercive action what ideally should come of free will, namely, good social behaviour. " Politics " literally means " what pertains to the city ", the laws of the city's life, particularly its good ordering for the well-being of every citizen. But the distinctive quality of political action is that it is compulsive action for the enactment and maintenance of law and order. Laws are made to be obeyed, maintained and enforced, and breach of them to be punished. The " State ", the organization of a community's life within a framework of law, is the one organization of society—parents and schoolmasters apart—which can use coercive physical force to compel obedience to its will.

Why should this power be given to it? Aristotle defined the aim of politics as " to provide the conditions under which men could live the good life ". The reason underlying the definition is easily perceived. There are so many tendencies at work in human nature, working out in the social or community life of men, which are inimical to the good life. Hence the task of government is to fortify the good, and restrain evil. St. Paul enunciated a similar doctrine in Romans 13, when he said that magistrates were no terror to honest men, but servants of God for their benefit; but to evil-doers, " avengers of wrath ".

Political action, therefore, is required to control inimical forces which make for social disorder and evil. These inimical forces may come from without the body politic, as from an enemy power seeking to invade and subjugate or destroy. Then the community is moved to defend itself by force, and war is the outcome. This situation was one of the springs of kingship as the seat of political authority. The king was the strong man who could lead the community in overcoming the evil disorder from without. Or the inimical forces might lurk within the body of citizens themselves, producing crimes and deeds of violence, acts of injustice and wrong, as between citizen and citizen or groups of citizens. Hence restlessness within the body politic, the cry for justice, for new laws to restrain fresh outbreak of evil or to express keener discernment of right— a continuous political ferment as evil made itself felt from generation to generation.

Further definition of the purpose of politics would be threefold: to defend life, maintain justice and advance liberty. These are tests of all good laws. They would justify factory acts, compensation laws, and social welfare legislation. Paradoxical as it may seem, a law to enact compulsory education must be judged right because it advances liberty: the liberty of the literate as over against the illiterate person. In some such way, President Roosevelt's " four freedoms "—from want and fear, to think and worship—can all be upheld as supreme concerns of politics.

That government is necessary and legitimate is therefore admitted, and its purpose recognized as good. Without it, human life would be utterly anarchic. This granted, some qualifications must be made as to the efficacy of political action. In the nature of the case, it is a second best. If men were not evil and sinful, the restrictive coercive action of law would not be necessary. Compulsion by law to restrain evil is confession of failure to constrain the good freely from within. In Christian terms, the state is necessary " because of sin ".

This sets limits to what political action can achieve. It

can compel outward conformity to law by fear and force; it cannot make a man good at heart. The genuinely law-abiding citizen is not so because the law compels him, but because he acknowledges that it is good he should obey the law. The rebellious law-breaker does not so feel. No outward power can compel him otherwise as long as his will remains his own. The one exception is when torture is applied, and the law-breaker's will is broken. The only effective transformation is that of inner constraint, as when a hardened Japanese criminal, who had defied authority and every officer of justice who had to do with him, was changed inwardly by reading the story of the Crucifixion in a New Testament left him by a prison visitor; and he who had seemed adamant before the power of the law went to the scaffold with the heart of a little child.[1]

Thus, though the purpose of politics is to restrain evil that good may thrive, it is incapable of achieving the good itself. For the evil it restrains is likely to persist: restricted here, it may break out there. It reappears with each new generation of mankind, and is likely to dog the human race till the end of time. This, in the language of the Hebrew sage, is the warfare appointed to man on the earth, the warfare with evil in the hearts of men continually breaking out into anti-social behaviour. Only the grace of God is adequate to overcome it.

This innate sinfulness, wherein lies the necessity of government, further limits the efficacy of political action because it so radically infects government itself. The perpetual riddle of politics is how it should ever be thought that sinful men were fit to rule their fellows. There have undoubtedly been wise and righteous rulers, and periods of good government, but they are few and far between. For the rest, the history of government makes sorry reading —a black record of folly, cruelty, wrong and evil. One has only to read Gibbon's mordant *Decline and Fall of the Roman Empire*, the story of Czardom in Russia, or the

[1] *A Gentleman in Prison.*

long, tortuous history of China, despite the wisdom of Confucius, to learn how blind, foolish and evil the governments of mankind can be.

Some doubt, indeed, whether the test of righteousness can be applied to government at all. Is not statecraft simply an art of reconciling divergent interests or using power to compel obedience to the will of the stronger? So Machiavelli or Hobbes would say. But that is to make politics what Thrasymachus in Plato's *Republic* said it was —the interest of the strongest—and to reduce it from a struggle for justice and the conditions of the good life to a mere rule of might, the strongest compelling his will, good or bad. This is to turn politics into that sink of corruption, absolute power. Whereat we recall Lord Acton's oft-quoted dictum: " All power corrupts, and absolute power corrupts absolutely."

II

These considerations should be kept in mind as we turn to look at the contemporary political scene, and particularly at the two conceptions of democracy, the rule of the people, to be seen at work in East and West. Mass electorates with free elections and choice between contending parties are token of the one. One party rule and minority government in the supposed interest of the working class characterize the other. In either case, political power is now in the hands of the common man, and the wide extension of governmental action and control so characteristic of our time is ostensibly to raise the standard of his life. How are we to weigh the worth of his new-found power?

So far as liberation has come to him, we ought to rejoice. In the past, the common man has had a raw deal. Grim wrongs have been inflicted upon him. He has, in myriads of cases, been both slave and serf, and endured the denial of every human right. He has been woefully oppressed and suffered unimaginable cruelties. He has been despised, scorned, trodden down and exploited. Ancient empires rode rough-shod over him, and forced him into labour gangs to build their pyramids and temples, and armed him for slaughter. The wars of the ages have devastated his home, ravaged his women-folk, and blasted his life and his hopes. He has been continually the victim of extortionate greed. That in our age he should have emerged, achieved power and won amelioration of his lot is a momentous fact of history. The victim of the ages now comes into his own. To some it will seem like the millennial dawn.

Nevertheless the rule of the people is fraught with formidable dangers, which ought not to be disguised. Government is a difficult art, and of all forms of government, democracy is the most difficult. The supreme virtues of state-craft are wisdom and justice. Where are these to be found among the people? How are they to learn and acquire political sense sufficient for the complex task of government? The virtues of state-craft are rare enough in kings and aristocracies: history is full of the follies and injustices perpetrated by them. But when kings err or act unjustly, they can be so tamed or disciplined that their power becomes innocuous, or they can be eliminated. Our own history tells of what happened to King John, Charles I or James II, as that of France the execution of Louis XVI, that of Germany, the ignominious fall of Kaiserdom, and that of Russia the nameless end of the Romanoffs. If aristocracies fail in justice, they too can be quelled, as in Britain by the slowly rising tide of mercantile and industrial power, or eliminated as in Revolutionary France or Soviet Russia by the ruthless act of the people.

But what are we to do when the people go wrong—err in wisdom, or act unjustly? They may do both. In this age of all ages, it will carry little or no conviction to say that the voice of the people is the voice of God. The voice of the people is the voice of the people and no more; they may utter folly and clamour for injustice. These things are as likely to happen as that kings have done foolishly and privileged classes have acted unjustly and for self-interest. The people so act within the nation and without, in internal affairs and in the affairs of nations. Democracy in practice is a reconciliation of divergent and competing group interests, particularly in the economic field which so often in our age dominates the political struggle. Thus in Britain, the struggle is less and less between employer and employed, but rather between differing groups of workers and the whole community, and balancing the claims now of miners, now of dockers, now of gas-workers, now of milk distributors, upon the common treasury. In America the White House has to wrestle with the diverse trade interests of the Eastern States, the Middle West and the Pacific sea-board, and to balance the demands of industry in the towns by the desperate plight of the prairie farmer. The economic and political follies of democratic groups are sometimes positively astounding.

The problem of democracy resolves itself therefore into that of achieving wise and just political actions. It is not necessarily to be at once discredited by its failure in this or that case to exhibit wisdom or justice. Democracy may have to learn by bitter experience, as men have always to do, and trust in the people must be prepared to pay the price, however costly, of their mistaken judgments.

Democratic government indeed is both delicate and precarious. Its characteristic in the West is that of decision reached after free discussion of the relevant issues. This takes place on two levels: the electoral level, by which governments are made or unmade, and the parliamentary level, by which laws are enacted. On the first level, we encounter the task of evoking, educating and mobilizing that mysterious and almost incalculable power, public opinion. Who can predict what will be the resultant of the choices of the thirty-four million men and women who now compose the British electorate? Will passion sway, or cool judgment? Will class interest prevail or wise discernment into the public good? The creation of a common mind and the discovery of principles of united action, are thus test issues for democracy. British democracy, for instance, is based upon majority rule and the two party system, with care for the rights of minorities. In practice this has meant two highly organized bodies of political opinion, advocating divergent principles and policies, submitted to an electorate, a portion of which is already committed to one or other side, and a portion whose judgment may be swayed, now in this direction, now in that. That latter portion has been the determining but incalculable factor in British politics. He would be daring indeed who would venture to say that that more indeterminate part of the electorate is always moved by either wisdom or justice. On some occasions, undoubtedly and unmistakably it has been so moved: on other issues, both folly and injustice were evident.

This statement, however, over-simplifies the question. Within the parties of the two-party system, as in Britain or the U.S.A., there are smaller groups with diverging tendencies. Sometimes these groups may break away and form new parties, displacing the old, as the Labour Party in Britain broke away from the Liberal Party. Or the case may be, as so often in continental democracy, notably in France and Germany, a number of parties, none representing an absolute majority of the electorate, all competing for power, subjecting government to kaleidoscopic change and thereby undermining the security and permanence of the State. In these divergences, the political competence of the common man is severely tested. Confusion and bewilderment are seen where we should look for clear judgment; division in counsel makes unity of action difficult or impossible, and the gospel saying receives new illustration: A house divided against itself shall not stand.

The crisis in democracy provoked by the struggle for power between divergent and opposing groups, whether divided by privilege or the lack of it, economic interest, political convictions or religious faith, may help to explain the stark new phenomenon of the totalitarian state parading itself in the democratic era as government of the people, by the people, and for the people. Hitherto democracy has striven for the balanced constitution, always guarding against power becoming absolute. Hence it has checked the power of administration by compelling it to answer to the court of the people in parliament, and making parliament answerable to the vote of the people, and while making parliament sovereign in making law, yet entrusting the judiciary with the responsibility of seeing that impartial justice is done according to the law without political interference. Democracy has sought to do this in order to liberate men from arbitrary power, and to keep the power of the State in check by the right of free criticism. Even in the struggle of divergent groups, none becoming supreme, a measure of freedom for minorities has been assured.

Nevertheless, both in the system of checks and in the unending and unresolved struggle of groups, a certain slowness and ineffectiveness in the political machine has been felt which has tended to make resolute men impatient with democracy so conceived, especially when it has been used to protect the claims of privilege and to withstand the extension of greater liberty to the common man. Hence the new phenomenon of the twentieth century: the seizure of power by a minority party, the sweeping away of antagonism, the reckoning of criticism or opposition as "reaction" and treason, and the exercise of state compulsion even over the inner sanctuary of a man's mind—all avowedly in the name and for the interest and security of the common man. Is it surprising that sensitive minds should see in this strange Nemesis of freedom a tyranny over the human spirit worse than that exercised by the medieval Church in the days of its greatest power, or should wonder if the common man, in his acceptance of this tyranny, is not exchanging the freedom of his soul for a mess of pottage?

This fresh emergence of absolutism in the world with the rise of the new regime in Russia is a feature of the modern political scene which occasions the greatest disquiet. It is an irony of history that after men have struggled to curb absolute power wherever it has reared its head—papal or ecclesiastical tyranny, absolute monarchy, tyrant classes and tyrant nations—in the interest of our common humanity, it should break forth again in the ambiguous guise of the "Dictatorship of the Proletariat". The tyranny of Czardom has been swept away, to give rise to that of the Polit-Bureau in the Kremlin. We must not be misled by the ostensible aim of raising the standard of life of the Russian people, nor need we decry the actual accomplishment in technical advance, use of the land, provision for health or education. The fact remains that it is power reposing finally in the hands of fourteen resolute men, with all the characteristics of absolutism: ruthless will, secret police and secret trial, suppression of opposition, elimination of people, individually and in the mass: a menace to the rest of the world. Perhaps the most striking demonstration of it is the claim to dominate expression of the spirit in literature, science and art. Where the minds of men ought to be most free, they are curbed and bound. This, it is claimed in terms of pure Marxist doctrine, is the only way to the perfect community on earth.

One further comment must be made. The common man is still divided against himself by interests of race and nationhood, as well as by divergent economic interests and political convictions. The world situation shows the nations of mankind struggling painfully from the anarchy of national sovereignties into world order and unity. How long that struggle will continue, and by what means solution will at last be reached, are questions no man can answer. Here one consideration alone claims attention. War and the menace of war still face the peoples of mankind. But now they must of necessity be democratic wars, wars of the people, and democratic wars are the worst of all wars. Hitherto we have had dynastic wars, imperial wars, religious wars and civil wars. We need not minimize

their horrors nor make light of the terrible memories they
have left behind them. In all of them accumulated miseries
fell upon the common man. But the evil of war took on a
new intensity when war became democratic, a war of
peoples. When national conscription was inaugurated by
the French people in the days of the Revolution, and con-
script armies, numbering millions, became a feature of
organized life in Europe, a new menace to peace came to
birth. The American Civil War, a democratic war if ever
there was one, was the most terrible civil war—except per-
chance the one that till yesterday raged in China—on
record. The First World War—though provoked by dying
imperialisms—was essentially a war of peoples : vast armies,
numbering millions, stretched from the North Sea to the
Alps. The Second World War is still more significant. It
was totalitarian war : to an extent unprecedented in human
history, not only the manhood, but the womanhood of great
peoples was mobilized for conflict. To that record of
terrible conflict was now added the deep foreboding and the
shame felt in the hearts of men by the invention and use of
the atomic bomb. In the hour of his emergence to power
and liberty, the common man is faced with greater danger
than has ever confronted him.

III

If our review of the current political scene is true, the
outlook for redemption by politics seems very remote. The
divisions in Western democracy and the menace of absolutism in the East promise no finality to the political
struggle. The former lacks a common or agreed faith on
which to build the new community, and while no one can
foretell how long the existing regime in Russia will persist,
the fate of previous absolutisms suggests that it cannot and
will not last for ever. Meanwhile the political problems
before the nations of meeting the elementary needs of food,
clothing and shelter for the increasing numbers of the race,

and building a world community amongst the peoples of the earth, will tax their sagacity and resolution for many generations. We shall have reason to be content even if here and there only we can make some advance in human solidarity and goodwill. Even so, over all the haunting question will arise: To what ultimate end? For the generations come and go, emerge on the stage of history, play their little part, and disappear as though they had never been. What is the end of the unceasing political struggle, and the meaning of man's life on the earth?

Once again the query is relevant: Has religion anything to say? More than once in this discussion we have had reason to reflect on the inadequacy of the view of human life which limits our existence to this world alone. If we are creatures of time and children of nature only, there is no more meaning in the economic or the political struggle than that of the trees in the forest, the bees in their hive or the ants in their nest. Neither individual nor race has any permanent worth or enduring existence.

But if, as the Christian religion affirms, men and women are born to be the children of God by creation and grace, and are children of eternity more than of time, a new light is cast upon the meaning of our temporal existence. It is then a preparation for a life that is eternal—in quality as in endurance—and our economic and political struggles are subordinate to that end. Religious faith can give deeper meaning to the dictum of Aristotle that the purpose of politics is to provide the conditions of the good life. Translated into Christian terms, the dictum reads: the purpose of politics is to provide the conditions under which men can live as the children of God during their temporary sojourn on the earth. No more and no less!

What that means in terms of the economic struggle the previous chapter has attempted to show. What it means in terms of our political endeavours—in the maelstrom of our political conflicts—it is more difficult to say. The interplay of religion and politics has a disquietening history behind it.

The attempts of religious men to exercise the art of government have not on the whole been more successful than
those of others. The way is strewn with the litter of failure
by theocracies, priestcrafts, papacies that usurped temporal
power, ecclesiastical statesmen, Churches that became subordinate to the State, and states which became subordinate
to the Church. The depth of ignominy was reached when
politics were embittered by wars of religion, and the
struggles of rival faiths accentuated the divisions of mankind! In such an impasse, men were easily tempted to
say: "What has religion to do with politics? Away
with it."

This unhappy issue was in part a reflection of the inherent
problem of politics, the use of compulsion to achieve the
good, and of the fact that like all else that is human, it is
infected by our innate sinfulness. Foolish, sinful and imperfect men—even though they be the best of their kind—
are not likely easily to make a success of governing their
fellows. Moreover, the corrupting effects of the exercise of
power are as likely to be seen in clerics as in other men,
and priests of the living God may fall into the sin of pride
or be lured by vain pomp. Thus it has been with the
Wolseys and the Richelieus of history.

Despite all this, the heightened intensity of the political
struggle when religion entered it reflected one inestimable
contribution that religion has to make to politics, namely,
that of responsibility to God for our exercise of power!
It partly explained the sharpened intensity of the conflict.
It meant that conscience had come into the matter. Men
now felt they struggled for what was right in the sight of
God. While on the one hand the sense of responsibility to
God could keep kings humble, and on occasion reduce
them to penitence—except when some extreme notion of
the divine right of kings held them in thrall—on the other
hand it could nerve humble men to loyalty to the right to
the bitter end, and uphold them in the struggle for liberty
of conscience. That *motif* runs through all the wars of

religion, and helps to relieve some of their more sinister aspects. That Catholics and Huguenots, High Churchmen and Puritans, should be divided we may deplore: that each struggled for the right as they saw it in a deep dependence upon God gave dignity to their struggle. Do not British democracy and the Labour Movement owe something to the fact that so many of their progenitors were God-fearing men?

If now we ask what may be the contribution of religion to the political struggle of the present time in Britain or elsewhere, this supreme principle of responsibility to God for our political acts comes first. To God, the things that are God's; to Caesar the things that are Caesar's—is a principle with divine sanction. But all things are God's, and only some are Caesar's. If the things which Caesar claims belong to God, then for the Christian God must be obeyed, and not Caesar. "Tell the King I die the King's good servant, but God's first!" was the last message of Thomas More to Henry VIII and it went from a scaffold.

There are two levels on which the principle has to be asserted. The first is on the level of action by the Christian community, the Church, in contact with the State. It is not for the Church to usurp the functions of government: that way lies disaster. The Church's function is prophetic, not governmental. That prophetic function it must discharge fearlessly, as Hebrew prophets did of old, yet with true discernment of the proper themes on which it can speak. Where injustice is done, where human dignity is affronted, where proper liberty or elemental right is denied to Church or people, and when the State intrudes where it ought not, east or west of the "iron curtain", the Church's voice ought to be heard in full sense of her responsibility to God.

The other level is on the plane of the individual Christian's participation in the current political debate and action. For in this day when political power has come into the hands of ordinary men and women, he is among those who have it in their possession and are responsible for their use of it. He cannot rightly divest himself of it. More than all others, he should know how to use it wisely, justly, disinterestedly and with a fine public spirit. Whatever part he takes in the debate, whatever service he renders in the political field, local or national, he should be clear as to the ends he should have in view as a son of the living God, not for himself but for the whole community. Social justice, care for man as man, and essential liberty will be his twin concerns, and to the best of his judgment and ability he will strive to serve both and to win others to do the same. To do that wherever public opinion is shaped and decisions are taken for the common weal, conscious that for every word and deed of his he is responsible to God, is no small contribution of religion to the struggle for righteousness in our day and time.

X

THE COMMON MAN, COMMUNITY AND CHURCH

LIFE FOR THE COMMON MAN, as for all others, is exhausted neither by economic necessity nor by the clamour of politics. Beyond these, there stretch other ties which bind him to his fellows, ties of home, occupations of leisure and the varied interests which fill his waking hours when work is done. This is the aspect of his life when, as he might himself say, he can relax and is free just to be himself, and can occupy himself as he will.

Does not the common man need religion here also, if he would fill these hours of leisure and relaxation to good purpose, in care for his home and in cultivating gifts of neighbourliness, friendship and fellowship? Experience shows he may easily misuse the opportunity which this side of life affords. If sins of one kind—sloth, greed, dishonesty and the rest—scar the world of industry, and lust of power darkens the world of politics, the leisure of mankind is disfigured by squandering sins of dissolute and profligate habits and sexual perversion, from which too the common man must be redeemed. Moreover, the dimensions of his life are not confined to the fellowships of earth: there is a fourth dimension which should impel his gaze Godward. If religious aptitudes and the sense of God are ever to be stirred within him, it is in his hours of leisure that they must be cultivated. The nurture of religion, whether private or public, is a leisure occupation. We need time, in Matthew Arnold's phrase, to possess our souls!

I

We here touch the community life of men in the widest range of associations which bind them together. In any given locality—village, town, city or nation—men and women are bound together, not only by economic interests within a framework of government, but also by ties of family, some semblance of a common faith or outlook on life, and by a variety of cultural pursuits. This is not to say that these varied interests are uniform throughout the whole community. They may be very diverse. Some men will be more religious than others; some will outwardly show no interest in religion at all. There will be variety in the cultivation of the arts; some people will follow literature, others music, others again the drama. Indoor and outdoor recreations, the hobbies men pursue, will be equally varied. In so far as the pursuit of one or other of these various interests draws men together, the community will be honeycombed with a variety of associative groups, and the sum total of them, together with economic and political interests, will constitute the ties which attach the common man to his fellows.

Of these associative groups, the family is generally more closely knit than the rest. A true community is a community of families, rather than an assemblage of individual persons. In the family, men and women are united by the marriage bond, held by ties of affection which bind them to one another and to their children, steadied by the responsibilities of keeping the home and holding the family together. In the modern world, it is true, the social function of the family has undergone a great change. Its function as an economic producing unit has almost disappeared except in agricultural communities, and even as an economic consuming unit is less than it was. It remains as a necessary biological and cultural unit of the greatest importance for which the claim may be confidently made that it is still the basic unit of society. When all is said and done, most of us are born into a family, and among the ties that bind us to our fellows are the ties of kinship. Children without a normal home life have recently been recognized as constituting a social problem of some magnitude, for whom the lack of parental care must be made up. Strictly communistic societies find the question of what to do with the family a very testing one, a touchstone of their power to achieve their goal. If they seek to disband the family or weaken its bonds, the relations of men and women become distorted, and the care of children a first charge on the community.

If the family tie be weakened, life is atomized, and the individuals of the family group are set adrift in that grim phenomenon of our time: mass society. In an older day members of a family often worked together at a common trade. Now more often each goes out to a different occupation, there to meet other individuals equally detached in working hours from their family groups. The forging of common personal interests in this situation is acutely difficult. In work and leisure nowadays, men meet *en masse*, in the factory, at the football match or in the cinema. True community is not easy in either. If proof be sought, watch workers from a factory, or spectators from a league match or people coming from " the pictures ", hasting on their several homeward ways!

Reflection on the first principles of community has not yet gone as far as has examination of the grounds of economic or political life. Economics and politics are much more precise sciences than sociology, the science of society, which is still a fledgling among the scientific disciplines. The subject matter of economics and politics may be complex, but the social links they investigate are fairly well defined. The study of society includes both economics and politics and much else besides, since it must investigate whatever social ties unite men. The growth of human societies from primitive tribalism up to the complex nation states of modern times thus becomes a fascinating subject of enquiry, which attracts some very acute and forward-looking minds.

Nor is it merely a subject of academic interest, but a most immediate and practical concern, which confronts us at every turn in the modern world. We face it whenever a great city corporation demolishes a slum neighbourhood and transfers the population to a new housing area. Here is enforced movement of population for peaceful and beneficent purposes, and not the grim dispersal of populations under the rude arbitrament of war. How shall the people taken from the congested parts of inner belt London or Manchester to Dagenham, Burnt Oak or Wythenshawe, forge the ties of community that will bind them together in the new habitation? How is a sense of community to be evoked which will weld together the people of the projected new towns of Stevenage, Crawley or Peterlee? Uprooted from old familiar haunts, how shall they take root in the new locality? Ties of association they knew are broken; how shall they fashion new ones? Religious and social workers who have battled with the problem tell us how acute and baffling it is. Amidst strange faces and fresh surroundings, however alluring the greater amenities, it takes time, perhaps a generation at least, for people to settle down to the new life and become a living community with real ties of attachment and something of a common outlook. It is almost as though we had set out to re-colonize Britain in a hurry. Our town and country planners have much to learn.

Nor does the problem emerge only in the creation of new communities: it operates in long established settlements of men. There is the immediate question how the people of a given community—a mining village in South Wales or County Durham or some West Riding woollen town—get on with one another, achieve neighbourliness and solve the problem of living together. Beyond that, there is the yet larger question how they will face the swirl of change that may sweep them to decay. For communities are planted, wax and wane, and the face of the earth is strewn with the litter of human settlements that fell on evil days and came to decadence or ruin. The new towns and housing areas of our time, after all, are the outcome of problems facing our old cities with their vast and unwieldy population swarms and overcrowded dwellings, evil legacies of an earlier day.

Nor is the problem one of local community alone. What forges the bonds of national unity, links the people of England, Wales or Scotland together, leaps the divisions of three races and makes the British people one? A common history, scarred by internecine strife out of which political unity was rudely hewn: growth of common economic interests and mutual flow of populations: a dominant language which steadily displaced native speech; and some semblance of a common though diversified heritage in faith, on which a common but equally varied culture was based—in these the factors of national community are discerned, not in Britain alone, but in many lands.

The problem, indeed, is world-wide, complicated and difficult. The U.S.A., for example, presents the historical spectacle of four centuries when many stocks of an ancient civilization migrated across the ocean to a new and almost virgin land, dispossessing the original inhabitants, to establish with much stress and strain a new community of mankind. A kindred problem, with some variants, faces Latin America. Europe, on the other hand, the home of many nations sharing the heritage of three ancient civilizations, is a grim picture of the disasters and upheavals which attend the community of nations through the iniquity of war, and illustrates how gaunt is the problem of rearing a stable community life out of the divisions of race. Within three short decades we have seen the elimination from history, probably for ever, of Esthonian, Latvian and Lithuanian nations, along with the attempted destruction of a whole racial stock and the uprooting and enforced dispersion of some millions of yet another race from lands which had been their ancestral home for generations. Will there ever be a settlement of Europe? If we turn East, we see ancient communities dissolving and taking new forms by the very urgency of ideas and social pressures derived from the West, upheaval taking place with almost volcanic revolutionary force. He would be a bold man who would forecast the future of the communities of mankind in Far East Asia, the mutual relations of India and Pakistan, the shape of the new China, or the ultimate outcome of the steady dispersion of Chinese people in Indo-China or Malaya. Who will eventually people the vast unpeopled spaces of Australia? Finally, there is Africa, whose community problem is possibly epitomized by the sharp tensions of South Africa over the relations of the white, black and brown races, vexed with terrible legacies of ancient wrongs and fears.

II

The achievement of community, whether local, national or international, does not, on this showing, appear to be easy of solution. Such community as is realized must be achieved, in the modern world at any rate, in the face of swirling and often disruptive change. Utopian dreams of evolving or creating a perfect state of society amongst mankind on this planet appear to be utterly illusory in such a situation. The record of history is so broken with failure and wrong, the future so uncertain, that a permanent ground of stability in the earthly scene seems nowhere likely to be found. Meanwhile life goes on, and the generations pass.

Yet a certain nostalgia for true community plagues the heart of mankind. There are few reflections more subduing than to contemplate how on the wreckage and ruin of an old life mankind sets to work to make a new home. People make their habitations still above the buried civilizations lying beneath the wastes of the Desert of Gobi, Arabs and Druses set up their camps by the mounds of ancient civilization in the Levant, and displaced Germans look for a place to make a home amid the rubble of devastated Berlin!

What accounts for the haunting cloud of failure that hangs over the community life of men? Man, we have heard with almost tiresome reiteration, is a social animal. That at least means that he cannot live as a human being, except in social relations with his kind. His birth, his physical growth, his mental and spiritual development, are all the outcome of social acts on the part of the others, and the interaction between him and them. He seems to be born, therefore, for community with his fellows, and cannot exist without it.

Yet for such a life, the raw material of human nature seems in itself imperfectly adapted. The three strongest human impulses are self-preservation, the sex-urge, and the herd instinct. But of these three, the last seems the weakest. The tie which binds us to our fellows, and makes us seek their society and fly for companionship within the crowd, may, in times of stress and strain, go down before the other two. If we seek another ground in human nature for fellow-feeling, impulses of sympathy, love and helpfulness, we have to seek it in awakened maternal and paternal impulses, and in the sense of kinship within the family unit. Yet, left to operate by themselves, even these may be fitful and uncertain. Fathers desert their offspring, and human mother-love is at times casual and evanescent. There is little natural sense of brotherhood, even between brothers kin. Esau and Jacob fall apart; cupidity and a disputed inheritance, or rivalry in love, may make them sworn foes. If this be true between natural brothers, it is even more startlingly exhibited by strife between communities. If war appeals to an heroic, generous and self-sacrificing strain in human nature in order to defend the common heritage, face to face with the foe it will break down all over-riding restraints, and let loose the native cruelty, sadism and lust of the savage heart of man.

What is the conclusion to be drawn from this review of human nature? If it is true, it utterly discounts those attempts to build a new order of society on a basis of the essential goodness of human nature or the innate justice, goodness and benevolence of men. The natural man, it would appear, is not so well adapted for community with his fellows as these optimistic views of human nature would affirm. The truth is rather with Jeremiah: " The heart (of man) is deceitful above all things and it is desperately sick "![1]

If this be true, then those whose trust is in the natural man, a mere creature of nature and time, are in sorry plight. The struggle for true community is not only unending from age to age, but in vain. It is then that we are driven to ask whether there is any resource in supernatural religion. If our hope is not in man, can it be in God? What if man, though born for fellowship, cannot find it in himself or with his kind, unless he first find it in God? Since the raw material of human nature is so imperfectly adapted for true community, is there any work or act of God, any approach of God to man, which can so transform and redeem a man as to fit him for a real fellowship of humanity in God?

We need not here beat about the bush. This is the Christian doctrine of redemption according to which the very power and love of God reach out to mankind in Christ, and are brought to bear upon unregenerate human nature, in individuals and groups, to transform it into new life. If this is accepted for true, a fresh valuation of man becomes necessary. He is not simply a creature of nature; he is a creation of God, born not only for time, but for eternity. Fallen and sinful though he be, there are still about him the bruised and broken marks of his divine ancestry. Within him, there is something that whispers of that from which he has fallen and bids him penitently aspire after fellowship with the God who made him. His

[1] Jer. 17.9 (R.V.).

very nostalgia after true community is a symptom of that *malaise*, the desperate inner unease, which makes him cry out for God, for the living God.

Some further observations sustain the truth of this view of our human situation, and point the way to a community of life centred in God. One merit of the Christian view is that it treats human nature realistically. The Christian religion is neither optimistic nor pessimistic about human nature. It takes it as it is: as sinful, and therefore impotent of itself to achieve the good. It takes it also as it is and may be, by the grace of God, born for better things and redeemable.

The ground of this faith and hope for mankind, however, is in God and not in man. The Christian religion not only requires a revaluation of man, but an interpretation of history as the story of God's search for man. Christian faith sees God unveiling Himself through the wonder of the world, in the gropings and dim perceptions of the heart of man, in the witness of the prophets and seers of all generations, until the consummate revelation in Jesus Christ, in whom the pre-Christian and Christian ages become one. The content of this revelation, which proclaims the nature of God who created and redeems us, is summed up in one word: Love, eternal in God, incarnate in Christ! Only in divine sacrificial love is the mystery of human existence made plain. Human history is the story of the pursuit of sinful man by the undying love of God!

> " Ah, fondest, blindest, weakest,
>   I am He whom thou seekest!
>   Thou dravest Love from thee, Who dravest Me! "

In the transforming power of Divine Love, when accepted into the heart of man, lies the secret of true community. It cannot be compelled from without. It must be freely constrained from within. Its efficacy is seen when it draws forth love to God, which overflows in love to men. Then, in very truth, the Kingdom of God appears amongst us. Of its power to disarm the evil in human nature and to evoke the good, history and experience give many examples. One must suffice: the testimony of Thomas of Spalato to the power of the preaching of Francis of Assisi: " The whole matter of his discourse was directed to the quenching of hatred and the establishment of peace. His dress was mean, his person insignificant, his face without beauty. But with so much power did God inspire his words, that many noble families, sundered by ancient blood feuds, were reconciled for ever."

III

Our final enquiry concerns the Christian Church. What has it to offer to the life of men in community? It should have much, for it is at once the creation and the custodian of the Christian Gospel, made to be the instrument through which the Love of God should reach the common man. The Christian Church, it has been well said, does not belong to those within it, but to those outside it. Ought not the common man to be able to look to the Christian Church to ease his nostalgia for true community?

Ideally, he ought to be able to do so. The Christian Church is a creation of Divine, Redeeming Love, and is a community intended to be the embodiment of that Love operating through its members. " By this shall all men know that ye are my disciples; if ye have love one to another."[2]

In practice, the answer is more ambiguous. The divine treasure of which the Christian Church is custodian is contained in " earthen vessels ". Redeeming grace works but slowly, and sanctification is a rare achievement. All Christians are " called to be saints ", but true saints are few and far between. Dante's characterization of our humanity within and without the Church in the *Divine Comedy* has profound meaning for us. There are impenitent sinners who, while they remain impenitent, are beyond hope.

[2] John 13.35.

There are penitent sinners, whose hope is in the purging, purifying influences of divine grace. There are the redeemed, aglow with the love of God!

We need not dilate on the imperfections of Christians which mar and hinder the witness of the Church, and frustrate its power to be an instrument of true community. Church history is scarred with the unlovely traits, sins and failings which have shadowed the Church's witness. Do we not know of proud prelates, ambitious and worldly priests, and fanatical preachers who have made the world grow scornful of religion? Have not love and fellowship often failed both within the Church and towards the world without? Is not the present divided state of Christendom an accentuation of other causes of bitterness and strife between men? And has the common man not ground for saying that sometimes the Church has been deaf to the cry of the oppressed and wronged, and dumb when justice was affronted or liberty denied?

All this may be true, and so far as true, is matter for deep and abiding penitence and renewal of life and love. But it is not all the truth, and the other side of the question should give pause to those who deny the validity, worth or relevance of religion, lest in rejecting the broken earthen vessel they also throw away the heavenly treasure. Despite its faults and failings, the Christian Church has a contribution to make to the community life of men, without which true community amongst men cannot be achieved. At all three levels of community life—local, national and international—the contribution of religion to community is indispensable.

To begin with, there is no tie so binding as that forged by sharing in common faith and worship. That has been proven in history and exemplified in our own time. For the sake of religion, men have sacrificed their economic interests, cut themselves off from their political attachment to native land or country, foregone their cultural heritage, and submitted to become wanderers on the face of the earth. Thus the

Huguenots of France and the Pilgrim Fathers of England.
The solidarity that held them together on their exiled way
was the solidarity of religion. Nor is it different with men
exiled for their faith from Russia, Poland, Czechoslovakia
or Germany in recent times. Their exile may be voluntary
or it may be forced: but the real compulsion is of religion.

Several factors contribute to this sense of solidarity in a
religious community. First, there is the awareness of God
which pervades the fellowship. "The Lord of heaven and
earth we found to be near at hand, and as we waited upon
Him in pure silence, our minds out of all things, His
heavenly presence appeared in our assemblies, when there
was no language, tongue nor speech from any creature."
So declared the Westmoreland Seekers in 1652. Any
devout and worshipping congregation could make a similar
assertion. Second, this invests their fellowship, and indeed
all their life, with the quality of sacredness. Here are
kindled the emotions of awe and reverence for want of
which life becomes secular and ultimately devoid of fundamental meaning. Once one saw a glow of awestruck
wonder on the faces of working men and women taking
Communion one Saturday afternoon in the Lady Chapel of
L'Eglise du Sacré Coeur on the Montmartre in Paris. The
wonder of the love of God was transfiguring their workaday lives. A kindred glow has been seen time and time
again on the faces of British Methodists—miners, weavers,
fishermen and the like—singing the traditional songs of
Methodism that have come down from the Wesleys.
Thirdly, out of the awareness of God comes a new sense of
belonging to one another. There is a community of life
between Christians, closest between fellow-Christians of the
same communion, but often enough giving Christians of
different communions a strong sense of solidarity as together they face a hostile or unbelieving world. It is
reported that W. E. Gladstone, High Churchman as he
was, frequently went to hold fellowship in the deep things
of God with a Methodist working man in Hawarden vil-

lage: and similar association between Dr. John Oman and Baron von Hügel is recorded from Cambridge. And once more, the influence of such religious experience is pervasive. It directs conscience, and shapes character, conduct and culture. It gives its peculiar quality to the Christian home, determines the Christian attitude to work, and makes the use of leisure purposeful over all its range, from rest and relaxation up to the delights of friendship and culture, inspiring voluntary service for the community and culminating in the joy of personal communion with God.

We can only briefly indicate the influence of the solidarity and pervasive influence of religious fellowship on local, national and international community. On the local level, test the influence of any alert and glowing religious fellowship on the community around it. "There are some exceptionally fine men in that church," was said of the Christian community at Wheatley Hill in County Durham with which Peter Lee was associated: "strong-charactered men with a bold social outlook," says Lord Lawson, when quoting the remark. There are whole villages and many towns in the British Isles which owe their moral fibre and their culture, their delight in music and drama, even their recreative pursuits to the churches and chapels in their midst, and this despite the measure of decline in the religious interest. On another side, we recall the strength of religious faith exhibited by a Christian village congregation in resisting tyranny in high places and in low, as set out by John Maarten in his vivid story of the Church conflict in Hitlerite Germany: *The Village on the Hill*.

The influence of the Christian community on national life is more difficult to measure. Its task is to be the conscience of the nation, the guardian of morals and the prophet of righteousness. If religion declines, moral standards are undermined, and men and women grow careless of truth, purity, honesty and goodness. Such things are possible when a people becomes too enamoured of material well-being and the things of sense, and loses touch with the finer things of the spirit. Moreover, there is a great peril to be faced on this level. There is such a thing as Christian patriotism, when Christians seek to achieve the best for their country, as part of the love they owe to God and their neighbour. But religion may sometimes be prostituted to serve the baser ends of an ignoble patriotism: and those in power seek to enlist the support of religion for ends which dishonour God and man. Then the prophetic function of religion must be fearlessly discharged.

On the international level, one consideration stands out pre-eminently. The universal Church of Christ has an indispensable contribution to make to world community. In much travail and pain, through actual conflict and with prospect of more, the nations of mankind are struggling into unity. One day a real community of nations may take shape on the earth. But the Church of Christ is itself a supra-national community, whose members and communions embody a fellowship which even now transcends distinctions of race, colour, language and nationality. You can trace a solidarity of Christian faith in all the great communions, uniting men of many races in one brother-hood of belief and life: be it Roman, Orthodox, Lutheran, Calvinist, Anglican, Methodist, Baptist or Independent!

Not that the Christian contribution to the community life of men is anywhere perfectly realized. Far from it. But enough is known, despite the frailties of Christians, to make more desirable. If a sense of community embracing mankind everywhere, and lifting the life of common men to its desired goal, is to be achieved, then the contribution of religion is indispensable. It is necessary, now, in the struggles of the present. It will be necessary to the succeed-ing generations while time lasts. In the immediate situa-tion which confronts the Christian Churches the world over, there is urgent need of new and adventurous experi-ments to establish contact with the common man wher-ever he is to be found. We made fresh discovery of that amid the upheavals and dislocations of war. Evacuation, air-raid shelters, the need of troops and the plight of refugees tested both willingness and capacity to offer fellowship to men and women in sore need of it. The need is not less in war's aftermath. The gaunt extremity of millions of displaced persons in various parts of the world will press upon us for years to come. There is not a locality in these islands which has not some community problem calling for Christian insight and effort, as a young minister wonderfully discovered in a faded suburb of South London. A new generation of youth needs to be helped to find its place in community in a very uneasy world. European workers who come at our call need to find a home amongst us, and coloured students and workers look wistfully for a welcoming hand. Factories and workshops begin to open their doors to the factory padre as a messenger of Christian community. Experiments like those of Dr. George MacLeod in the Iona Community, and the work of Father Groser at St. Katherine's Dock exemplify the need and point the way. The common man needs God and the Christ who reveals Him.

That is the conviction in which this book is written, stronger at the end than at the beginning. Beatrice Webb, in *My Apprenticeship*, tells how she turned at the crucial point of her life from the service of God to the service of men! The antithesis is a false one. The love and service of God are the springs from which, for the Christian, issues the call to the love and service of men. " I loved the people," said Henry George, " and that led me to Christ as the people's best Friend and Saviour." " And I loved Christ," replied Cardinal Manning, " and that led me to the people for whom Christ died." Therein lies the real hope of the common man. Without the redeeming love of God, his hopes for this world are vain, and he will have none for the next.